Conquering College

The most fun you can have
learning the things you need to know

Written by
Howard Scott Warshaw

Illustrated by
Jennifer B. Brabson

Editing and layout by
Karen J. Kellerman

Cover design and layout by
Howard Scott Warshaw and Karen J. Kellerman

Back cover photograph by
Kathryn A. MacLean

Published by
EduQuest Corporation
P.O. Box 610787
San Jose, CA 95161-0787

Printed on recycled paper.

Dear Bonnie's Gister, May all your Conquests be this pleasurable. Enjoy!)

EduQuest Corporation
P.O. Box 610787
San Jose, CA 95161-0787
(408) 441-7355

Slag Procrastantine and Edmund St. Vincent Polyurethane III are fictional
characters and are the exclusive property of EduQuest Corporation. Any
resemblance to real persons, living or dead, is unintentional and purely
coincidental.

Printed in the United States of America.

First printing 1992

ISBN: 0-9635111-0-6

This book is printed on paper made from 10% post consumer waste
and 50% recycled fibers. Every page is entirely recyclable.

To Sara and Sophie

To Sara

Who
On a cold Philadelphia night
Sat with me at the old wooden table
Sipped her ever present hot water
And talked me into going to college
At a time when I was leaning toward not.

To Sophie

Who
Represents the greatest disappointment of my life
She missed all the good stuff

Acknowledgment is a wonderful thing . . .

In the beginning, Uncle Bruce said "write that book." Although he was not the first to say this to me, he was the first to make me listen. Books don't get written until they're started. I have him to thank for the start.

Write exactingly. Write swiftly. Write by experience. Write under duress if you must. But you can't write in a vacuum. I had many readers during the production of this book. Fortunately for me, they were the right readers. I haven't an adjective sufficiently superlative to adequately express their contribution. Will the names do?

First there were the students. Thank you to Christine and the brothers Ahn. Thank you to Vonny and Ben and the aptly named Reed. Carrie and Charlton deserve a special thanks, and this is it.

Next up were some graduates. Steve, Ed, and Neelesh donated their valuable time and feedback. June and Tom and Doug and Wink (love that name) were generous and forthcoming not only with their expert criticism, but also with their college experience. Even my Dad went through it with a fine toothed comb (and let's face it, without him this book would never have been written).

A seemingly endless series of Karens and Jennifers were involved with this book, which is incredibly ironic for reasons I won't discuss here. I would like to mention one of each.

Jennifer gave the pictures, and got the picture. A lot of learning went on during this project. That's what books are all about. This book is immeasurably better for her contribution to it.

The moment I first laid eyes on Karen, I knew she would edit this book. What I did not know was that she would also form and sculpt it so masterfully. Her dedication and diligence on this project were matched only by the enormous value of her friendship throughout. Karen is a consummate professional.

I am proud to be the author of this book. Had it not been for Jennifer and Karen, I would never be able to say this. The two of you have given me a very special gift. You made my dream come true.

Contents

Who am I to tell you? * I am not a genius * I developed a system * Why did I invent this system? * What about you? * What is college? * What is a student? * What is a professor? * Uncle bruce was right * Why choose this book? * How you should read this book * A point of style

What RASABIC is * System foundation * What RASABIC is not * There you have it

Why read ahead? * How it works: Reinforcement * How to do it: Using goal directed behavior * The expository students: Slag and Edmund * The start of the term * Once again

Editor's Note

When Howard started writing this book, he knew he wanted to have it edited professionally. He approached me when I was a consulting writer at the high tech organization he worked for. I was convinced his ideas for conquering college were insightful and well-developed; however, not knowing him well then, I had my doubts about his ability to write pure informational material.

My doubts were unwarranted. In fact, I was the one with much to learn. At first, I was a grammar fiend, criticizing little things such as sentence fragments and slang words. I felt it was important to set a sound example of good English grammar. After several lectures by Howard on "impact writing," I realized I needed to read the book differently. What would otherwise be unacceptable *would* work here. Those sentence fragments are significant vehicles of emphasis and impact, and colloquial language places author and audience on common ground.

Howard's style is conversational, and it's almost as though he is still a college student himself. He introduces imaginary students with real-life experiences and ambitions. You'll recognize yourself in one of them. The system Howard establishes is founded on some very fundamental concepts. His tips and pointers go beyond the standard advice you will find in other books about college.

I have great respect for Howard and his work. I wish this book had been around when I was preparing for college. I encourage you to pay attention as you read *Conquering College*. It is dedicated to providing valuable insights that will make the ideal college experience a reality.

Karen J. Kellerman
Vintage Publications

Preface

People in our culture have been going to college for quite a long time. Yet the perception of the *process* of going to college has changed little in all that time. It is still viewed as getting an education.

Many other institutions in our culture (marriage, mental health, personal finance, and sexuality to name a few) have also been around for quite a while. But these activities have undergone a tremendous amount of scrutiny over time, and the perception of them has changed accordingly. Very dramatically in some cases.

Compare attitudes about sexuality. Over the last thirty years, the amount of literature and attention devoted to sexuality has increased remarkably. Consequently, sexual attitudes have been changing significantly since 1960 and they continue to change. There is no question that paying more attention to something is likely to result in changing it.

What's interesting to me is that college has never received this kind of scrutiny. I can understand why sex has, but I do not understand why college has not. One would think that the education of our future leaders and decision makers would be worth some of the grant dollars that are currently spent on studying worms' mating habits and chicken worship.

People track SAT scores and starting salaries of graduates, distribution of major subjects and correlations of ethnic groups and grade point averages. But very little attention has been paid to the process of getting through college successfully.

Many people have published the classic stuff about studying under good light, sitting with good posture, and paying attention in class. No one has addressed the nuts and bolts issues of going to school: How can I influence a teacher to give me a better grade for the same work? How can I organize my schedule to reduce my work load and still carry more classes? How can I be a more efficient student so my results and my fun time both increase?

I did these things in college. I wrote this book to share my secrets with future students and perhaps start the focus of attention on "the process" of going to college. An area that many people today complain about but few honestly address.

This book deals with the reality of going to college. Not the euphemisms and platitudes, but the mental, political, and perceptual factors that go into succeeding in college. It will teach you not only how to study, but how to use that information to your advantage before you ever walk in to a test. How to get a teacher to the point where you will get credit for totally contrived answers because you have made the teacher so sure you understand the material they will countermand their own doubts. I have done this.

The easiest final I ever took was one that I was excused from. That's right. I was excused from some finals and got A's in those courses. I can teach you how to do it also.

This book discusses serious issues with a rather humorous slant. Don't let the humor distract you from the real messages inside. The things you will read about go on all the time in college. By becoming aware of them you will have the opportunity to take advantage of them. If not, you will just be another head of student cattle.

If you would like to feel more in control of your college experience, then go ahead and start turning pages. If not, that's OK. All I can tell you is good luck in the stampede.

Me & You & College   *1*

Who am I to tell you?

I conquered college.

By this I mean: I received my Bachelor of Science degree from Tulane University (in New Orleans) with honors, sporting a cumulative GPA (Grade Point Average) of 3.9. I completed a double major in Economics and Mathematics, with an additional minor in Theater Arts. You will see evidence of all three throughout this book.

I was on the Dean's list every term, and was recognized as a Tulane Scholar. I was inducted into the freshman honor society, the math honor society, and Phi Beta Kappa, the national honor society.

I did all this in three years—not four—saving lots of money.

On the strength of this record, I was granted a full scholarship to the school of engineering where I completed my Master of Computer Engineering degree in one year (GPA 3.9).

Then I hit the job market with a vengeance, earning over one million dollars before my 27th birthday (honest, you can check my tax returns). I worked exclusively as an employee, at jobs which I received primarily on the strength of my college record.

Would you be proud of these accomplishments?

I am. My college record has been, and will continue to be, a constant source of pleasure (and profit) in my life. I'm always pleased to discuss it with anyone who is interested. My parents and relatives don't care if you're interested; they will tell you about it anyway.

You see, my parents were not only proud, they were also quite relieved. Before college, I had never been a distinguished student. I got mostly B's and C's from kindergarten through high school.

Which brings me to a very important point:

I am not a genius

I am not a genius.

It's so true, I said it twice. My aptitude test results prove it. Intelligent? Yes.

Genius? No way.

Officially, I'm not even gifted. About the best that can be said for me is that I am above average and kind of weird.

That places me right smack dab in the middle of the college crowd since most of the people who contribute to my above-average-ness never bother to go on to college.

So how did I do so well in college?

I developed a system

High school never appealed to me primarily because of my belief that it wasn't important. Don't get me wrong; the basic reading, writing, and math skills are absolutely essential.

Beyond that, however, it seemed high school had very little to offer me, so I didn't put much into it. Consequently, I was not a very adept student by the time I reached college.

When I arrived at college, I realized that college *was* important. So I worked my butt off in my freshman year. When I saw a C on my first test in college, I worked even harder. I studied all the time.

I earned a 3.78 GPA in my freshman year. I was very satisfied with these results, but my overwhelming impression was that I had worked too hard. There had to be an easier way. There had to be a way to do as well or better, and have more fun.

Before my sophomore year began, I started working on a new approach. I started budgeting my time more effectively and learning how to study more efficiently. A few weeks into my sophomore year I started to party.

I did not party to escape. I partied because I was confident extra study time was not necessary to make my grades. By the middle of my sophomore year I was partying every night. Every night! (By the way, the word "party" means taking time to do whatever you want, and not think at all about school. Everyone has their own way to party. The question is: Do they have the time?)

I overloaded my schedule with extra courses and, with the exception of the first few weeks of each term, still partied every night. I finished that year with a 4.0 and enough extra credits to take a few courses during the summer and return in the fall as a senior.

My system was working. I was getting the hang of being a college student. The simple ideas I started with before my sophomore year blossomed into elaborate theories and techniques. I developed a complete system for getting the best grades in college with the least amount of effort. My system allowed substantial free time during the rest of my Bachelor's program, and all the way through graduate school. I used this free time either to relax and enjoy myself or to work for extra money.

Incidentally, that 3.78 for my freshman year was the lowest annual GPA in my entire college career.

This book teaches my system.

Why did I invent this system?

There are three great motivating forces behind all inventions. The two that got me were fear and laziness.

I was afraid to fail in college. College *is* important. I knew I needed a distinguished college degree to achieve my goals.

I also realized I was neither a genius nor a very good student. This also frightened me. How could I succeed in college without the tools necessary to do so? Other successful students appeared to work all the time. I was very lazy and could never do that much work for four or five years. Their way wouldn't work for me.

So, accepting my fears and laziness, I knew I had only two options: Forget about college, or invent a better way to do it. A way that could work for me.

You are no doubt wondering about the third great motivating force of invention. It's libido (you will certainly learn this in college).

What about you?

Yes, you. We're in this together.

There are three big assumptions I make about you throughout this book:

Assumption #1:   You are ready to be an adult.

Being an adult does not mean giving up all fun in life. I am an adult, and I have a lot of fun. Being an adult means being responsible for yourself and your actions. That's all.

The only person who makes you succeed in college is you. Know why? Because no one else cares. If you cut classes and blow off your work, no one will care. The administrators and professors won't dislike you and they won't condemn you. They will simply flunk you and be done with you. They are educators, not baby-sitters. They have plenty of other things to do.

If you can accept and face the simple fact that your success or failure is entirely in your hands, you are ready to be an adult.

Assumption #2:   You want to do extremely well in college.

You know what this means.

"If you cut classes and blow off your work...
...they will simply flunk you and be done with you."

Assumption #3: You can accept a new point of view.

You've been in school for a long time and have many ideas about what school is like and how you should approach it. This book will challenge some of those ideas. Keep an open mind as you read the explanations.

Some people are closed-minded. They stick to their own ideas, spending time and effort trying to justify them. It takes less work and is more productive to consider new ideas and approaches, rather than defending old ones. This approach worked for Thomas Alva Edison, Marie Curie, George Washington Carver, and millions of others. It can work for you too.

Remember, we do things the way we do because we haven't figured out a better approach yet. People who think they already have the best approach will never improve.

If any one of these assumptions is wrong, don't waste your time. Throw this book away before you hurt yourself.

If they are correct, read on. You will not be disappointed.

What is college?

Stand in an empty classroom. What do you see?

Nothing, it's just a room. It isn't a college classroom until a bunch of people assemble there and make some agreements. College is a collective agreement among people. When everyone gets together and agrees that professors have authority, students have responsibilities, and each person will play his or her role throughout the term, then you have college.

College is a miniature society. It behaves politically. Human nature dominates and rules the situation. This is your greatest asset.

This book delves deeply into human nature. We will talk about you, your professors, and your classmates.

You will begin to understand yourself and those around you. Then you will use that knowledge to succeed in college.

What is a student?

A student is a person whose job is to attend college. A student is a *matriculator* (the college name for student). The goal of matriculation is to receive a college degree.

Going to parties, getting a tan, and taking road trips with friends are nice extras in college, but they have nothing to do with being a student.

The first and foremost priority of a student is to be a student. Students who lose sight of this don't do well.

This does not mean you will never do anything but study. It means that your priorities should always be clear when deciding what to do next. Just keep in mind while you are attending college that you are a student first and everything else second.

What is a professor?

A professor is a person with a Ph.D. who has too much to do and not enough time to do it.

One of the duties of a professor (by no means the only one) is to rate you on your performance as a student. This has surprisingly little to do with your learning anything. The professor's job is merely to report your grade to the Dean's office.

Most of what professors are evaluated upon has nothing to do with teaching. They do research, publish papers (publish or perish!), and spend a lot of time playing departmental politics, which can make them very moody on occasion.

What you learn is up to you. The professor will present material, then look to you for evidence on which to base your grade.

Professors like it if you learn something, but they are not responsible for your learning. They are only responsible for failing you if you supply no evidence of learning.

As you will learn, supplying evidence of learning and actually learning are two different things. Fortunately, this system enables you to do both.

Uncle Bruce was right

Before I left home for college, I asked my Uncle Bruce if he had any college advice for me. This is what he said:

"In college, if you get good grades, you have a good time. A lot of people goof around a lot and seem to be having a good time, but by the end they are very unhappy. The people with the good grades wind up the happiest."

He knew, because he was one of the goofers. The next several years of his life were a great disappointment. Ultimately, he decided to correct his mistake and go back to college, which lead to his next pearl:

"It's tough to go back to college."

Going back to college was a tremendous struggle. He succeeded because he learned from his earlier mistakes. Now he is doing quite well, but he will never be able to reclaim the years he wasted between his first half-hearted attempt at college and his second sincere one.

Get it right the first time. College can be of great benefit to you, but only if you do it right. The first time isn't easy, but it is the easiest.

Why choose this book?

This is not the only book about going to college. There are many. Some are written by teachers, some by students, and some by advisors. They are good books, but they tend to cover the same basic points. They give you the standard advice on how to study and make grades, but very little explanation of how it actually works.

Conquering College explains in great depth what other books only mention. It also covers many new and powerful techniques you simply won't find anywhere else (at least not before publication of this book).

Other books cover many extraneous topics that have little to do with your success in college. What to pack for college, and doing your laundry are things you will certainly deal with, but you can figure them out for yourself.

Too many pages are spent on these ideas at the expense of valuable knowledge that can help you directly in college.

Conquering College has one focus: Enabling you to graduate with the most impressive degree possible in the shortest possible time, using the least amount of effort, and having the most fun.

Another thing I find distressing about other books is the lack of qualifications presented in these books. It is very rare for the authors to say exactly how they did in college. Not unheard of, but rare.

You have seen my qualifications as a student. I have also been a teacher at the high school, college, and business levels. I have, without exception, received very high ratings on all teacher evaluations.

I can do *and* I can teach. Those are my qualifications.

This is *Conquering College*. This isn't like the other books. Other books tell you how to get through college. This book tells you how to GO through college. Like a buzz saw.

How you should read this book

On first reading? From start to finish. Don't skip around. Each chapter builds on material presented in the previous chapter.

This is a new approach to being a student. There are new terms and ideas. If you skip the background, you won't understand what you are reading.

You will not be able to use this as a reference book until you understand that to which it refers. Read it straight through once, then skip around.

There is also some genuine college vocabulary in this book. If you come across a word you do not understand, check the glossary. The glossary is located conveniently in the back of the book for your edification and reading pleasure.

A point of style

I worked very hard to make this book interesting and fun to read. Yet the system it teaches is very intense. This is not a contradiction, it is merely a style. A style intended to help you learn.

There are many important points presented in this book. They are often presented in a humorous fashion, but that doesn't make them any less valid or serious.

This is my teaching philosophy: The best way to get a point across is to make it both clear and amusing. After all, if something isn't enjoyable, how excited will you be about doing it?

There are people who don't approve of this style. They believe information must be lifeless or joyless in order to be worthwhile. Here is my advice: If you can't take your information with a little bit of humor, perhaps you are taking things a little too seriously. Let me refer you to my favorite quote (which I learned in college):

> "Please don't mistake my levity for shallowness any more than I mistake your gravity for depth."

You're going to learn how to conquer college, and you're going to have a good time in the process.

Relax, turn the page, and open your mind.

The RASABIC System

2

What RASABIC is

RASABIC (pronounced RAY-sah-bik) is a system for achieving maximum results with minimum effort in college. There are three key components to the definition of RASABIC: system, maximum results, and minimum effort. Look at these one at a time.

Systems

First and foremost, RASABIC is a system. A system is nothing more than a bunch of tools working together to achieve some purpose or goal.

A transit system is a bunch of tools. There are roads and tracks and train cars and busses and stations. They all work together to provide a system to accomplish the goal of getting people where they need or want to go.

Your body is a system. It is a big system. It is a collection of systems that work together to accomplish the Herculean task of being you. The basic tools are muscles and bones and veins and organs. These tools work together to form sub-systems like the digestive system and the circulatory system. All these systems are combined to form you.

The RASABIC system is a collection of tools and sub-systems. If you're worried that you don't have the tools, don't be. If you can read and write and speak, then you have all the basic tools necessary to implement RASABIC. You need only learn how to use them. That"s what I will teach you.

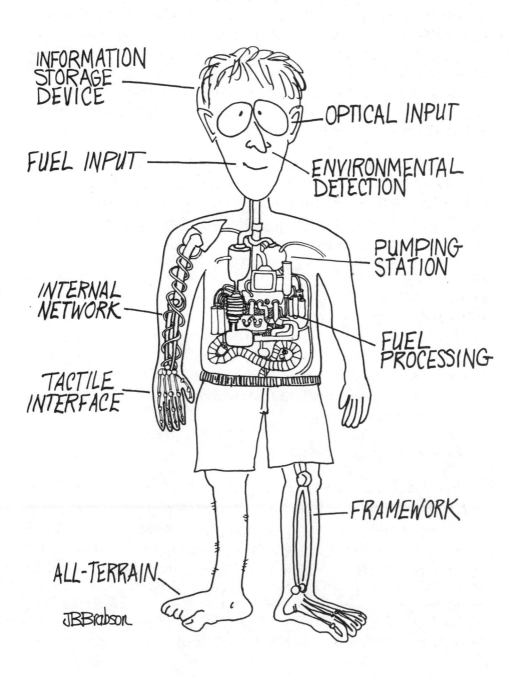

INFORMATION STORAGE DEVICE

OPTICAL INPUT

FUEL INPUT

ENVIRONMENTAL DETECTION

PUMPING STATION

INTERNAL NETWORK

FUEL PROCESSING

TACTILE INTERFACE

FRAMEWORK

ALL-TERRAIN

JBBrabson

"Your body is a system."

Maximum results

RASABIC achieves maximum results. Maximum results means more than just getting good grades. Maximum results means learning the subject matter you are studying, and more importantly, retaining more of the material that you learn!

This is crucial. There is a tremendous amount of redundancy between lower level and higher level courses in most curriculums. The more you retain from lower level courses, the less studying you will need to do in higher level courses. That will leave you more time for enjoyment.

Retention also makes a tremendous difference at the most critical and stressful point in the school year: Finals. The RASABIC system enabled me to do less studying during final exams than at any other time during the term. This drove my classmates nuts.

While people were running around the dorm wired out of their minds on caffeine and speed, I was reading for pleasure and going to movies. They hadn't slept in two or three days. I slept like a baby.

They were trying to make up for a term of neglect. I knew my material cold. They were stressed out, pissed off, and just plain scared. I was calm, cool, and confident. Which mental state would you prefer to bring into a major test?

Minimum effort

RASABIC requires minimum effort. There are many paths to any particular destination, but very few require minimum effort.

Think of opening a door. You will use one hand to push the door open, but you are free to choose where to push. You can push on the handle side of the door, or you can push on the hinge side of the door. Both ways will open the door, but pushing on the hinge side takes a lot more effort and strength than does pushing on the handle side. The result is the same, an open door, but the amount of energy expended varies dramatically.

By knowing where, when, and how to apply your energies, you can always accomplish a goal with the minimum effort. That's called being efficient—getting the most out of your efforts.

RASABIC will make you a more efficient student. It teaches you the where, when, and how of college. RASABIC will keep you pushing on the handle side of the education door.

A system for achieving maximum results with minimum effort. That is RASABIC.

But wait, that's not all. RASABIC is also an acronym. It wouldn't be much of a system without a good acronym, would it? RASABIC stands for:

Read
Ahead,
Stay
Ahead,
Be
In
Class

That certainly sounds simple, doesn't it? Of course it does. Most things seem simple in principle. Don't confuse simple with easy.

Running a marathon is simple. Just put one foot in front of the other for twenty-six miles. It's simple, but it's not easy.

As you look deeper into this simple principle, it becomes more involved. The marathon runner is concerned with more than each step. She considers diet, clothing, technique, and terrain.

RASABIC is a simple principle.

Read Ahead so that you are familiar with the material ahead of time. You know where the pitfalls are.

Stay Ahead to maintain your edge and provide a consistent level of mastery and participation.

Be In Class to cash in on these efforts. This is the most involved and the most important part. Be In Class means much more than just showing up. The classroom is where most of your benefit will come. Almost all of your outside work is designed to pay off in class. You cannot reap those benefits if you are not there.

There is much more to using these strategies than just saying them. RASABIC is not easy, but it's not terribly hard either. It's a lot easier than running a marathon, and it's a lot easier to learn than it is to develop. Believe me.

System foundation

RASABIC is built upon a big concept. An enormous concept. A concept that, once mastered, will virtually guarantee you can get anything you decide you want in life. Wouldn't you say that's significant?

This is the concept that enabled me to cruise college. This is the concept that made me a millionaire by the age of twenty-six. OK, here it is, the concept of:

Goal Directed Behavior

Goal Directed Behavior means that once you settle on a goal, everything you think, do, say, eat, drink, or sleep is directed toward achieving your goal. Everything.

This concept goes by many names: focus, concentration, desire, ambition, will, and even obsession. There is no force as irresistible as a person who is completely and totally focused upon the accomplishment of a specific goal. All martial artists understand this concept, much to the chagrin of many boards and bricks.

Everyone has the capability to perform goal directed behavior, but very few do. It isn't easy to do because life is full of distractions. Distractions interfere with goal directed behavior.

*"Those who maintain their focus in the face of distractions
succeed in the attainment of their goal."*

Those who maintain their focus in the face of distractions succeed in the attainment of their goal. Those who are sidetracked by distractions have their energies dissipated. They lack the force and strength to follow through. Successful athletes know this all too well.

Goal directed behavior has four elements: trade-offs, priorities, discipline, and awareness.

Trade-offs: Effective use of time

Life is a trade-off. Heard that before? It means you can only do one thing at a time. Whatever you choose to do, you do so at the expense of doing anything else at that moment.

Every day and night there are thousands of things to do. You can't do them all. Each time you do something, you make a trade-off. From all the possibilities, you choose one and do it. A trade-off is a choice.

In college, you are faced with a seemingly endless series of trade-offs. The trade-offs you make determine whether you succeed or fail in college. How will you make your trade-offs?

Priorities: Taking aim

You need a consistent basis to make these trade-offs and stay on track toward your goal. You do not want to make these trade-offs randomly. Goal directed behavior is totally non-random.

There are two primary ways to make trade-offs: preferences and priorities. Preferences are feelings. Priorities are decisions— decisions we make about how to handle our trade-offs.

Successful students use priorities to make trade-offs. Floundering students use preferences to make trade-offs. That's why they're floundering.

Preferences change both rapidly and frequently. They can change in any direction. Preferences are random. If you use preferences, you will introduce a randomness into your trade-offs that will lead you into chaos. You'll have to struggle to achieve your goal because you are fighting both the school and yourself. You will be a student divided and you will surely fall.

Priorities are stable (or should be). Priorities ensure that the trade-offs you make consistently contribute to your success. Each step you take brings you forward toward your successful graduation. Never sideways, and never backward. Priorities keep you on target.

I will not give you priorities. Only you can do that. I will help you set them. Once your priorities are set, you will be able to trust them and rely upon them. They will save you a great deal of time and energy. All you need do at that point is stick to them. That brings us to the next point, discipline.

Discipline: Staying on course

Discipline is a loaded word. That is to say, it carries many connotations. The mere utterance of the word "discipline" conjures up many vivid and powerful images. For the majority of us, most of those images are quite negative.

Because of this, we tend to experience resistance at the very mention of the word. Well, don't do that.

Discipline is not a bad word. It is not even a negative word. It is a word that has many shades of meaning. Unfortunately, we tend to focus on the negative ones.

In Webster's New Universal Unabridged Dictionary, the deluxe second edition (one of the few places where success comes before work), there are six different definitions for discipline, and that's for the noun form alone. Here are the first three definitions of the word "discipline:"

1. "Training that develops self-control, character, or orderliness and efficiency."
2. "The result of such training; self-control; orderly conduct."
3. "A system of rules or methods, . . ."

Nothing negative here. These are the definitions on which we will focus. Self-control. Character. Method. Use discipline to consistently and continually apply your priorities to your trade-offs.

Using discipline does not mean becoming an automaton who works all the time and never plays. Using discipline means you consistently work toward your goal.

Part of your goal is to enjoy yourself. As you will see, having fun time is an integral part of the system. One of the major applications of discipline in RASABIC is to ensure that you get enjoyment time on a regular and frequent basis.

Any system that does not account for fun time will never work for people, at least it would never work for me.

Awareness: Making your own luck

> *Success is a mixture of luck and skill. You must first cultivate the skill necessary to take advantage of opportunities. It is then a matter of luck as to when those opportunities arise. Some people work very hard all their life and never get their big opportunity.*

This is a popular definition of success. It is not entirely correct.

It is true that skill is a very important part of success. Without some basic knowledge and capability, no opportunity can be exploited.

It is also true that hard work alone does not guarantee success. You cannot succeed without some hard work, but the only thing that working hard *guarantees* is that you will get tired.

The erroneous part of the definition lies in the assumption that luck determines when, and to whom, opportunities come. That is garbage. Opportunity abounds. Opportunity is all around you, all the time.

How often have you heard about people making millions on simple little inventions or gimmicks? Think about hula hoops, post-it notes, and pet rocks. Have you ever said to yourself: "I wish I'd done that?" Of course you have, just as I have. So why didn't you?

You either didn't perceive the opportunity, or you saw it and didn't follow through. The opportunity was there all the time, waiting for any person with the awareness to take advantage of it.

Awareness converts day-to-day life into an endless series of opportunities. And here is the best part: awareness is not innate or genetic. Awareness is learned. You can learn to become more aware. As you do, you will see all the opportunities that elude your peers. Awareness is the difference between working hard and working smart.

Trade-offs, priorities, and discipline form a solid basis for the system, but a system must be applied to be of any benefit. The better the application, the greater the benefit.

Awareness enables you to recognize opportunities to best apply your energies. Awareness will let you achieve the maximum return on your investment of time and effort in RASABIC. Then you will be the one making people say, "I wish I'd done that."

Let's recap the elements of goal directed behavior. Trade-offs are the decisions you constantly make as you go through college. Priorities are the criteria you use to make those decisions. Discipline keeps you from straying off the successful path. Awareness helps you apply your energies most effectively.

Graduating impressively is a goal. Goal directed behavior is the way to accomplish a goal.

What RASABIC is NOT

RASABIC is not a trick. It is not cheating, and it is not magic. Above all, RASABIC is not a get-out-of-work-free card.

When I say RASABIC gives maximum results for minimum effort, don't make the mistake of thinking that minimum effort means no effort! There is a great deal of effort necessary to succeed in college.

Minimum effort means you will spend the least amount of effort to achieve the maximum results. This is because RASABIC will enable you to work at your highest efficiency, which means you will have the most free time possible and still excel in your studies.

You are a resource. RASABIC enables you to allocate yourself in the most efficient manner possible to achieve the maximum benefit from this resource (yes, I really did have an Economics major).

There you have it

RASABIC is a method for you to apply your energies in college so they bring you the maximum possible return for your time invested. Face it, your time in college is every bit an investment. It's an investment in yourself.

RASABIC is a simple system, deceptively so. Its simplicity masks some very powerful concepts. Use it well. It is one key to success that will open many doors.

The remainder of this book explains the ideas of RASABIC and how they work for you. Everything you will need to take full advantage of the system is here.

As I explain the techniques and concepts of RASABIC you will see, as I have, that it is a powerful tool for the college student.

RASABIC is the sword with which you will conquer college.

"RASABIC is the sword with which you will conquer college."

Read Ahead

3

Why read ahead?

You have memory. You have short term memory and long term memory. It is very easy to put things in your short term memory. It is very easy to forget things from your short term memory. Some things you don't forget. They are in your long term memory.

The object of study is to get information into your long term memory. Cramming will not do this. The object of cramming is to stuff your short term memory. Do you have an incredible short term memory?

There are two principle ways of getting things into your long term memory: reinforcement and trauma.

Reading ahead will enable you to use reinforcement to get your course work into your long term memory. Forget about trauma. You've probably had enough of that already.

Here is the main point of reading ahead: If you read and study your material in advance, you will retain the information you need to know. The lectures will reinforce that information and lock it in your brain, and it sure feels relaxing in there.

How it works: Reinforcement

An infinite amount of stuff happens all around you, all the time, yet you retain very little of what you see (or hear). Why do you select and remember the few things you do?

While standing near a busy street, you see hundreds of cars go by. Which ones do you remember? You might remember one you want or one that looks like your friend's car. You might even remember a car that resembles one that nearly hit you. The point is, you remember the cars that relate to your background–those with which you connect.

You *see* everything, but you only *retain* the things with which you relate or connect. You pick out and retain things that reinforce your background.

By reading ahead, you give yourself the background necessary to connect with the lecture. Since you have the background, the lecture can reinforce it. Boom! Retention kicks in. Your brain opens up and files that material away. It's automatic. You can't help it.

By attending class unprepared, you lack the glue to catch the lecture. The words go in one ear and start looking around for something to relate with or connect to, something to reinforce. Finding nothing, they express their disappointment: "This place is dead. Let's get out of here." They hastily exit out the other ear, leaving nothing in their wake but wasted time and an empty head.

Reading ahead gives you the glue to make that lecture stick in your brain.

This is rather abstract, perhaps an example would help. By George, here's one now:

You're sitting in class. You have not read ahead. The professor is lecturing on a topic which you are hearing for the first time. She begins, "Today we will cover the assigned reading . . ."

You have a vague idea of what she is saying, but it's all new and unfamiliar. You cannot relate. You are desperately scribbling notes, copying anything she writes on the board.

You are writing so much, you are not hearing what is being said. You are getting the notes, but missing the explanations. You don't even know which parts you understand because you don't have time to think right now.

The professor stops to ask for questions. You feel too embarrassed to ask, "What was the part after 'Today we will cover . . .'?" So you say nothing and hope you are not called upon to answer questions.

You feel anxiety and distress. You can't wait to get out. Won't this class ever end? Your mind starts to wander. It has to. Your mind won't stay in a bad place very long.

"Attending class unprepared. Words go in one ear and...
hastily exit out the other."

You just blew a lecture. You might retain ten or fifteen percent of the material, maybe. Later, you will go back and try to learn that material for a test. That lecture will not help you. You wasted that hour of lecture, and it takes more than an hour to reconstruct it. You could be out having fun with this time. You feel the resentment building.

Class makes you feel bad and inadequate. That is a very negative association. If you feel bad darling, you look bad. Looking bad is the first step toward scoring bad. You are on your way. Down!

Sounds kind of depressing, doesn't it?

Go back through the example, substituting "Howard" for "you" and making the grammatical adjustments. Now what you have is my high school experience. Not very pretty, is it? That is why I never cared much for high school.

Many students don't care much for college, for precisely the same reasons. But hey, I'm not trying to bring you down here. I'm just telling it like it can be. Now I will tell it again like it can be:

You're sitting in class. You have read ahead. The professor is lecturing on a topic which is fresh in your mind. She begins, "Today we will cover the assigned reading . . ."

You know exactly what she is saying because it isn't new. It's familiar. You can relate. You are taking occasional notes as she writes on the board.

You are not writing very much. You are listening carefully to what is being said. You are getting the notes *and* the explanations. You understand what she is saying. Often you know exactly what's next. The lecture is reinforcing the important parts of what you read.

The professor stops to ask for questions. You know precisely what to ask. You have seen the material and know what you are missing. You are eager to answer questions and show your knowledge.

You have confidence. You can feel the information locking in as it connects. Your mind is so focused, you are surprised when the class is over.

You just maxed a lecture. You will retain eighty-five to ninety percent of the material. In your long term memory! Later, you will go back and review this material for a test. That lecture will still be there. Your review is brief and relaxed. You already know the material. You can go out and have fun with this time. You feel great.

Class makes you feel good and competent. That is a very positive association. If you feel good darling, you look good. Looking good is the first step toward scoring good. You are on your way. Up!

Sounds kind of uplifting, doesn't it?

Go back through it, substituting "Howard" for "you" and making the grammatical adjustments. Now what you have is my college experience. Pretty, isn't it? That is why I loved college.

Not many students love college for precisely the same reasons. But hey, you could. The choice of scenario is entirely yours. This concludes the not-so-subtle-repetition-for-impact portion (yes, I really did have a Theater minor).

How to do it: Using goal directed behavior

Reading ahead means studying and learning the material as you read. Use discipline and awareness. Reading ahead does not mean skimming a few pages while waiting for class to start.

The first step in reading ahead is getting your text books. If at all possible, do this before classes start. Make a point of finding your books early. You can use the bookstore, a syllabus, or your teachers. Find out. Then get those books. The lines are shorter before classes start. The people who put it off are the ones who don't get books when a class is over-enrolled. They go on the wait-for-reorder list.

Classes get overbooked just like airplanes. You don't want to fly standby for your textbooks.

The book preview exercise

Having acquired your books, the next step is to become acquainted with them by doing the book preview exercise. Here's how:

Read the table of contents thoroughly. Understanding the words and phrases is not important; seeing them and briefly pondering them is. Take a few minutes. Do it slowly and concentrate.

Now start skipping through the book. Stop every thirty or forty pages and read a few random paragraphs. Odds are you don't understand what you are reading. That's OK, understanding is not the point here. In fact, the point is to remember that you don't understand.

What?

That's right. The point is to use your awareness and take your lack of knowledge to heart. This is an important process. You are programming yourself for positive reinforcement later.

Go on, pull the other one.

I'm serious. By doing this exercise, you plant seeds in the fertile crescent between your ears. These seeds grow and bear fruit as the term progresses.

Sooner or later you come to these ideas again in your course work. When you see them this time, you understand them because you now have the background to understand them. At this moment, a wonderful feeling comes to you in a pristine rush. You remember not understanding this idea, and you realize that you just learned something. You lose your knowledge virginity.

You experience the joy of learning. It's very satisfying. You may want to smoke a cigarette. That is what college is all about (the learning, not the smoking), at least from an educational standpoint.

You will luxuriate in this feeling more often than your classmates because you laid the proper basis. By doing this book preview exercise, you create many opportunities for this to happen, so it happens many times.

You spend an extra twenty or thirty minutes for each class and make the whole term more enjoyable. Good deal.

Did you acquaint yourself with this book?

Effective reading

To read effectively, you need five things: discipline, a translucent highlighter, a pen or pencil, awareness, and of course, the book.

First you need your discipline. Psych up to spend some real time here. You are about to improve your mind. Appreciate it. It's exciting. You are exercising your unique privilege as a human being.

Start reading. Use the highlighter to pick out summary sentences and key phrases in explanations. Don't highlight everything. Pay attention. If you read carefully, the key passages will jump out at you.

By way of definition, highlighting means using one of those goofy markers to paint certain passages in your book a different color. This makes them stand out like Darth Vader in Munchkinland.

If your highlighting is done well, you should be able to go back through a chapter, read only the highlighted parts, and get all the important information. It makes a quick and handy review, and it ensures that you only read the whole text once.

Use your pen to record questions as they arise. Save them in your class notes and ask them at the next lecture. It is very important to focus on what you don't understand, and clear it up. Also write your observations and thoughts in the margins, particularly when they add clarity to the text. The book is not the master. You are a team. Work together.

Lastly, use your awareness to stay focused. Sometimes you will be reading and suddenly notice that you completely missed the last few paragraphs. You read the words, but your mind was wandering and you don't remember a thing about them. Stop right there!

Go back to the last paragraph you remember and go through those passages again. Stay aware. Stay focused. Don't sleep while you read. Above all, don't continue reading until you either understand what you have seen so far or have written down the questions that will help clear it up for you.

A textbook is a house of cards whose top is the final chapter. If you miss some of the bottom cards, the entire house will tumble. If you need to, take a break. A short break. Use your discipline to maintain continuity.

As you read the text, make sure you are understanding what you are reading. You won't understand everything the first time you see it. I certainly didn't. Persevere. If you keep after it, you will get it.

But wait, that's not all you get. By spending serious effort in your reading, the difficult concepts will become significant to you. Significance is an emotion. You will develop an emotional stake in understanding these concepts.

This is great. This means when you do finally understand a difficult concept, the reinforcement of the relief will lock it in. You will retain that information because you worked hard to understand it. Again, this is automatic. It works for you with no additional effort. It is called "unearned increment"—in other words, a freebee.

Retention is a big key to learning college courses, and reinforcement is the key to retention.

"Don't sleep while you read."

Because you read ahead of every lecture, you will rarely see anything completely new in class. After the first fifteen percent of your term, you should be at least one or two chapters ahead of the professor. That's slightly over one week for a quarter, and about two weeks for a semester. Go for it. In the coming pages, I will show you many other advantages to reading ahead. Reinforcement is a tremendous benefit, but it's just the tip of the benefit iceberg.

Always remember this: The majority of your undergraduate career is spent learning things other people invented. Inventing this stuff is the tough part, and it's already been done. It is presented to you in a step-by-step manner. All you have to do is learn it. Here is a cute way to put it:

> I mightn't sail through every course,
> But never do I flunk it.
> For mine is just to learn the stuff,
> I never have to thunk it.

Think on this too: All the college's resources are there to make it easier for you. Use them throughout the term. These resources are only scarce at midterms and finals. You won't need them then.

The expository students: Slag and Edmund

There are two kinds of people in the world. Those who divide the world into two kinds of people, and those who don't. I frequently do.

There are many kinds of two kinds of people. This book focuses on two kinds of students: those who use RASABIC concepts and those who don't. Here comes an example of this kind of bifurcation (isn't that a great word) (don't ever be afraid to use good words) (especially in college) ("don't be afraid of parentheses either," he added parenthetically).

Let's meet two students.

Slag Procrastantine

Slag will not read ahead. He has better things to do. There are beers to drink and babes galore. Slag sees college as the moment his life has led up to. His own private playground with no restrictions, and the party light is on. Hey Slag, why aren't you reading and preparing for class?

"Are you kidding? I got all term to do that stuff. I'm a pressure player and a cramming machine. I didn't come to college to book it and waste my valuable youth.

"I'm going to have a good time all term. Then at the end, me and my good buddies Ms. Caffeine and Mr. Speed are going to pull it out. You'll see. Until then, Parrrrr-teeeeeee!"

You will see many Slags at the beginning of your freshman year. They will thin out dramatically by your junior year (not from speed, from flunking out).

Slag will scream at you to be quiet when you haven't said anything. This will happen around finals, when Slag is spending too much time with his good buddies.

Edmund St. Vincent Polyurethane III

Edmund reads ahead. He is doing better things. Edmund sees college as a means to an end, not an end in itself. He wants to do his best, get out into the real world, and start to succeed. Hey Edmund, why are you reading and preparing for class?

"Are you kidding? I want to do well here. I don't want to be one of those pathetic guys in a lousy job who is still trying to finish a decent degree at age 35.

"It's a tough job market, but there are always good jobs for top people. I'm going to have options when I graduate.

"Oh, by the way, don't let the name fool you. I am not a snob and I am not a dork. And call me Eddy, please. God I hate this name."

Edmund—excuse me, Eddy—is into the flow of collegiate success. He is focused on getting a good start. Eddy doesn't have buddies like Ms. Caffeine and Mr. Speed. Eddy's buddies write recommendations, not prescriptions.

Slag Procrastantine

Edmund St. Vincent Polyurethane III

Slag and Eddy may seem exaggerated to you, but you will see them around college. There are many more Slags than Eddys. The majority of people you see are neither Slag nor Eddy. They are somewhere in between. They are the herd.

We'll be seeing more of Slag and Eddy. Each is fun in his own way, but only one will wind up happy. You can guess which one, can't you? I knew you could.

The start of the term

In the beginning, there are parties. There are beer bashes, wine and cheeses, orientation get-togethers, fraternity and sorority rushes, and dorm mixers. People are running around getting introduced, welcomed, initiated, oriented, registered, redirected, and sloshed. Everyone asks the question: "What's your major?" What an opener.

You have the opportunity to waste a tremendous amount of time in all this excitement. I recommend that you don't.

Many people will tell you to ease in to it, to pace yourself and build gradually. That's good advice for drinking, but not for academics. Don't ease in. Dive in!

Do pace yourself, but start fast and ease off gradually. Psychologically, that is much easier on you. Here's why:

Let's assume that, like me, you don't enjoy the idea of doing a lot of work. The prospect of heavy work bothers you. It makes you uncomfortable. It should also be fair to assume that if you want to ace a course (instead of merely passing), there will be at least some heavy work involved.

You will do some hard work. When will you do it? By building gradually, you must be putting off that hard work until later. That means for most of the term you will be dreading that upcoming period of hard work. You won't be doing the work, but you will be dreading the work. There is a little black cloud in your head that rains on your parade. Day in and day out.

You are also putting off the benefit of that hard work. The "Be In Class" chapter will show how.

RASABIC says do it up front. Get ahead, right in the beginning. You will work harder in the first two weeks of the term than at any other point. That means for most of the term your hardest work is behind you. No little black cloud. You feel liberated. It also means you benefit right from the start. You don't waste any time and you get the greatest return for your work.

Remember the house of cards analogy? What you are doing is building a solid foundation. Do you know anything about house repair? If the foundation is OK, just about anything can be fixed reasonably. If the foundation is weak, the whole house is in jeopardy. Not many students understand this.

Parties make good study breaks but lousy occupations. Use hard work to establish a solid foundation right up front. It insures the term. Now, any other mistake is reparable.

For instance, suppose you underestimate the amount of work necessary to ace a course. If you wait, you will only find out when it's too late. You will have a B or lower in that course for the rest of your life because you failed to guess correctly.

If you start fast, you can adjust along the way and still hit your target. You can guess wrong and still ace the course.

That's insurance no company will sell you. It's available only from Mutual of RASABIC.

When Slag arrives on campus, he knows he's in the right place. What do you think, Slag?

"Pinch me dude, this is radical. This is like Nirvana, Valhalla, and hog heaven all mixed together. Shaken, not stirred.

"I now understand my purpose in life. I have meaning. I drink, therefore I am. Hey, I wonder if the Philosophy department has bashes like this, that could be my major major."

Slag is into it. Don't stand between him and a keg. You will not see Slag without a plastic beer cup in his hand for at least two weeks, even during classes.

When Eddy arrives on campus, he starts to see opportunities. What are you going to do now, Eddy?

"I'll tell you one thing, I'm not going to Disneyland.

"First I'm going to walk around. Get the feel of the place. Find registration, the book store, and the movie theaters. Then maybe check out some of the parties for a little while.

"Then I might hang out at the dorm and meet some people. Find out where my mailbox is, and when I can get my courses and books. You know."

Don't you want to party your brains out first with Slag?

"Well, not really. I mean, I like to party and all, but these afternoon things seem pretty dead. There are lots of things I need to find out first. Besides, everybody knows the best parties are at the frats at night. I'm going to get some stuff done now. There'll be plenty of action later on."

Eddy is still going to get his party time in, but he will also get some necessary things done first. He is establishing a successful pattern right from the start. As you will see later, that is when it counts the most. Eddy is just a RASABIC kind of guy.

Once again

☆ By now you have received enough reinforcement on the concept of reinforcement to understand its importance.

☆ You see how reading ahead provides the basis for this reinforcement, enabling you to trap your course work in your long term memory.

☆ You know how to preview your textbooks, and how to read them carefully for maximum retention.

☆ The first few weeks are the hardest, but the rest of the term (including finals) is easier.

☆ You have met Slag and Eddy.

Stay Ahead

4

It is now a few weeks into the term. You are ahead of all your classes. The initial lectures have established in your mind a firm basis for the term. You are sitting pretty.

You have three options; stay aggressive and increase your lead, ease off and maintain your lead, or drop everything completely and watch your lead evaporate.

If you choose the last option, you'd better start practicing eating pages instead of reading them. The information won't help you and the roughage will do you good.

Obviously, only the first two options are worth serious consideration. Either stay aggressive and increase your lead, or ease off and maintain your lead.

Staying aggressive sounds attractive. You are already on a roll, so why not keep rolling? You could finish the term's work about halfway through and cruise the remainder. Doesn't that sound good?

Perhaps. Here are two reasons that the wisdom of this approach is questionable.

Reason number one: It is important to be ahead, but getting too far ahead may be dangerous. When you are too far ahead, you are putting a lot of distance between the initial learning of the material (reading) and the reinforcement (lectures). That may be risky.

When you have an operation in a hospital, you are not prepped on the 3rd for a procedure on the 28th. The same principle applies to reading ahead.

The studying is crucial, but the system depends on combining the reading with the reinforcement. The reinforcement is what locks the material in your brain. Try to keep the information fresh. A two-week lead is optimal.

Reason number two: Although staying aggressive sounds good, how does it feel?

The first few weeks you are working very hard. That's good. That's why you're here. You are getting the benefit of your hard work, but you are also getting tired.

The light that burns brightest burns quickest, and the light that burns out casts naught but darkness. In other words, if you burn out you will blow it. Students who push too hard push themselves over cliffs and out windows. Both figuratively and literally. It's true.

Here is a lovely addition to your college vocabulary: *Defenestration*. Look it up. When you know what it means, you will keep looking up, especially while walking around campus during finals. Every year a surprising number of college students choose this as their final project.

You won't. You won't need to. Grinding yourself into academic pulp is not what RASABIC is about.

Remember, we are looking for minimum effort, maximum results, and maximum fun. That should tip you off that staying aggressive is not the preferred approach.

The RASABIC approach is to ease off and maintain your comfortable lead. You have worked very hard for two or three weeks. Now it's time to stop working hard and start working smart.

Reward yourself by easing your workload. Take a bit more relaxation time at night. Enjoy the freedom you earn.

Here's an idea: Think of your brain as a light bulb. It takes a great deal more energy to turn it on than it does to keep it on.

Most students only turn it on twice per term; once during midterms and once during finals. They don't bother keeping it on the rest of the time. You cannot read by the light of most students' bulbs. They are operating at minimum efficiency, and their records show it.

RASABIC says: "Turn it on once. Turn it on brightly. Turn it on early. Then simply keep it lit."

Staying Ahead means keeping it lit. Studying at your highest efficiency. Minimum energy consumption for maximum results.

Spending time

How and where you spend time is an important part of everything you do. In college it is paramount.

Time utilization is the central concept in Staying Ahead. You will organize your time to make the job of staying ahead as simple as possible.

There are three things that will come in handy for this task; trade-offs, priorities, and discipline. You remember these from Chapter 2; now let's use them to build something.

Generally, I like to approach things positively, but when discussing how to spend time in college, I find it easier to look at things to avoid.

The black holes

Do you know what a black hole is? A *black hole* is an astronomical phenomenon in which matter is compressed to such an extreme density that it generates an incredible gravitational field. Nothing can escape its pull, not even light. That is why it's called a *black* hole. Anything getting within range of that gravity will be pulled inexorably into the void, never to be seen or heard from again. Poof. Gone.

A black hole is nature's greatest sucking machine. It's a galactic vacuum cleaner, and no one can empty the bag.

Needless to say, you should avoid black holes while attending college. This will not be a problem. If a black hole shows up on campus, believe me, your worries are over.

What should concern you is what will happen if a black hole doesn't hit campus.

We have been discussing cosmological black holes. They won't be a problem.

However, there are black holes on campus that *can* be a problem. They are the time-wasting kind (scientific classification: *Timesuccus Flushmaximus*). There are limitless opportunities to fritter away your time for little or no benefit in college. They are all around you. Anytime, and all the time.

Here are a few of these black holes. Know them. Recognize them. Be not sucked in by them.

Bull sessions

The mother of all time wasters–and the most alluring–a *bull session* is when two or more students get together spontaneously and chat about anything and everything.

Bull sessions give you the feeling that you are socializing, getting the inside scoop, making friends, gaining popularity, and using your education. All in one neat little bundle. This is an illusion, but it's not a problem.

Bull sessions are also a lot of fun. This is a problem. There is a lot of pure enjoyment (and some good information) to be had with these informal get-togethers or extended phone conversations.

A bull session is like a philosophical argument. You can go back and forth, again and again for an endless period of time. Then at the end you can say "So what," and you are right!

Bull sessions are light hearted enjoyment, very refreshing, and often stimulating. So what's the problem?

You're walking to the library to do some research and studying. Oh look, there's Mookie and Suki. They are involved in a very poignant discussion concerning topics of grave import (this week). They call you over to ask your opinion and settle a point.

You have your own insights to add and are happy to lend this assistance where it is obviously needed and appreciated.

Five hours and seven beers later, you all say "so what," and head off in your respective directions.

Now you think what we all think after a major detour: "What was I going to do? Oh yeah, the research. Ah, I don't feel like it now. Oh well, $&%@ it."

That's the problem.

I'm not saying that you should go on and study. That is not where discipline comes in. Besides, you're in no shape to study anyway.

The place for discipline is at the beginning. The satisfaction achieved in that five hours could easily be had in two.

The thing to do is ask Mookie and Suki where they will be later (you know where that is already because they are there every night) and join them after three hours of study.

You'll get your work done, and whatever you missed during the first three hours can be filled in with a quick "so what."

There is no bull session that can't be missed. Selecting one as important is like focusing on one particular snowflake in a blizzard. Stay inside and do your work, then go out and play in the snow.

The dead zones

There are two periods of time that nearly everyone kisses off: The time between classes, and the time after last class but before dinner. Who made this rule?

By "between classes," I do not mean the ten minutes after your 10 o'clock class and before your 11 o'clock class. I mean times when there is at least one full period between classes. Use that time.

The best thing to do is the homework of the class you just finished. The next best thing is reading or reviewing for your next class.

Start doing whatever you would do at your next study session. After all, it is an hour of study time you have on your hands. If you do it now, you won't have to do it later. Can you think of something else you'd like to do with an hour this evening? I thought you could.

The same thing applies to the gap between last class and dinner. Many students take the "cocktail hour conversation" as a sacred rite, and they exercise it daily.

This is also an important prelude to the twi-night bull extravaganza. Don't sell yourself short. If you're good, you can kill a whole day.

Try it both ways if you like. Use the time effectively for two weeks and enjoy a great deal of guilt-free free time at nights.

Then switch for two weeks. Enjoy goofing around during these times and doing your work at night, however long it takes.

At the end of four weeks, go back and compare the value of the goofing time as a trade-off for the evening free time.

You're a smart shopper. Do whichever you enjoy more. Compare and save!

My advice is to study now, not later. Besides, night life doesn't happen in the afternoon, and usually it doesn't even start until quite late.

Lingering

Lingering is a nice name for loitering. Lingering happens at many times: after meals, after movies, after classes, after breaks, after tests, and ever after. In fact, the only time it doesn't happen is before something.

Lingering is standing around and shuffling your feet and half talking to people before going on to doing something useful. It is a semi-bull session that can easily blossom into a genuine bull session. Lingering is procrastination.

Don't linger. Be pointed. Be focused. Respect your priorities. You have things to do and places to go. Go and do them. Why linger?

Do what you need to do, then be equally aggressive doing what you want to do.

Lingering is limbo. You are a student, not a dancer (unless, of course, you are a dance student, in which case limbo is not only a good idea, it's a requirement).

"Lingering is procrastination."

TV: The ultimate test

When I graduated from high school, I had watched more TV than any of the kids in all those studies. I'm talking an average of six or seven hours a day, more on vacations and weekends. I loved TV.

I went cold turkey at college. I held myself to four hours a week, including Monday Night Football (hey, some things *are* sacred).

The only way I was able to do this was to keep my mind focused on my goal: Do well in college.

I used my priorities and discipline. I found more productive interests to fill my time, like developing this system.

TV will not help you do well in college, unless you have video tapes of all your professors in compromising positions. If that gives you any ideas, keep in mind that it is extremely difficult to compromise a college professor.

These are but a few of the myriad ways to waste time. College students are bright and creative people. They come up with the most innovative and outlandish time-wasting schemes you'll ever waste time watching.

Time utilization is a very important part of RASABIC. You don't need to remember that. Just remember that the time you waste (or don't) is your time, and it's the only time you've got.

Homework

Homework is the third event in the triple crown of reinforcement. Read ahead to get the information. Attend classes to lock it in. Then do all your homework to hermetically seal the material in your brain. Optional or not, do your homework.

It won't take long.

Homework has two functions. It is used to review material already covered and to introduce the next material. In either case, you have already done this work.

Homework becomes an exercise in validation. It's confirmation that you know what the professor wants you to know. This validation is very positive. Enjoy it.

Some professors will actually count the homework as part of your grade. This is free money. If there is anything in college you can max out, it is homework. Don't let it slip.

There is also homework you assign yourself.

There will be times when you have all your assignments completed, you are ahead of every course, and you are suffering from the illusion of having nothing to do.

Review!

Any night when you have no other pressing work to do, review material from your courses. Spend ten or fifteen minutes to look through your notes, or read the highlighting in your textbook. Do this for four courses. That's one hour or less.

Do something every night. It doesn't have to be much, just something to keep in the habit. Then go out and have a good time.

Extra credit

You are going to have free time. RASABIC will ensure that. You are not required to ignore your studies during this time. It is simply an option. Another option is doing extra credit work if the professor offers.

Do all the extra credit work you can. It will be additional reinforcement for you (can't get too much of that), it will impress the professor, it won't hurt your grade, and it could result in a big time payoff!

Yes, big time. Don't laugh.

What's the easiest final you could ever have? The answer is the one you don't have to take.

I was excused from the final exam in one of my courses. Because of quizzes, tests, and extra credit, I had enough points that I could skip the final and still get an A for the course.

The professor informed me of this, and of the fact that he didn't need another paper to grade. I didn't argue with him.

That only happened once, but there were similar experiences in other classes. It was frequently the case that I did not need to ace the final in order to ace the course.

Do you think that relieves pressure? Do you think that makes a final exam less stressful? Do you see the value of doing extra credit?

Staying ahead is Y. I. P.

This does not mean that staying ahead is the reason I relieve my bladder.

Y. I. P. stands for Your Insurance Policy.

Hey, stuff happens. You get sick. Somebody dies. You have a once-in-a-lifetime opportunity to go somewhere for a week, or maybe you are selected as a contestant on a TV game show. Sometimes you just need a break.

The unforeseen happens without notice. That's why it's called the unforeseen. Surprises pop up. You do not know when, or if, they will occur.

When surprises do happen, there is usually no time to prepare and plan. By staying ahead, you give yourself a built-in cushion against disaster.

You can't guarantee surprises will be pleasant, but you can guarantee they won't make you fall behind in your course work.

Keep the good times rolling

Make sure you have fun in your spare time.

That may seem like a ridiculous thing to say, but when you become truly goal directed and focused, it is surprisingly easy to forget about entertainment and relaxation.

It is not necessary to become a study-holic. There is no Students Anonymous.

You can participate in extracurricular activities, earn some money, go to parties, read for fun, do ice sculpture, or whatever you want. Just make sure the things you do are fun for you.

There will be some enjoyment and satisfaction in the first few weeks of the term, but there will not be much free time. There will be a lot of hard work. It is important to know there will be consistent and frequent relaxation periods once you enter the meat of the term.

These breaks will continue for the rest of the term, including finals week. This is the interest you collect on your substantial time investment at the beginning.

Collect that interest! It will keep you fresh and motivated.

This advice is for the dedicated student only. To Slag, this is a silly idea. Hey Slag, how do you motivate for study?

"Motivate for study? Bogus, total contradiction here. Studying is, by definition, demotivating.

"When you say motivation, I think of the three B's: Beaches, Bars, and Babes. Now *that's* motivating.

"I'll get my studying in later. For now, would you mind moving a little, you're blocking the rays."

Slag does not see fun and relaxation as a departure. To Slag, studying is the departure.

"Don't stand between Slag and a keg."

Eddy is focused on study and achievement. Eddy, how do you motivate for study?

"That's a strange question. I don't think of myself as motivating for study. I am here to study. It's not a task to me, it's a purpose.

"More accurately, it is one purpose."

You have others?

"Well, yes. I'm going to get a degree that will take me places after I graduate.

"I want to learn a lot while I'm here, but I don't intend to let that interfere with getting good grades and graduating. Learning and making grades are two different things. I intend to do both."

Eddy, are you for real?

"Of course not. I'm a fictional character."

Sorry. What I meant to ask was: Are you sincere?

"Oh. Absolutely. Although there are many opportunities in the fictional world for people without degrees, I may want to become real someday.

"The real world has little use for mediocre grads, and even less for those without any degree at all."

Once again

☆ Staying Ahead means using your time effectively. Doing less work to maintain the lead you've established.

☆ Efficient time use avoids the black holes: bull sessions, dead zones, lingering, and TV.

☆ Homework and extra credit can yield significant savings in both effort and anxiety.

☆ Staying Ahead is insurance against your worst enemy, the unknown.

☆ Don't lose sight of your own entertainment needs.

Be
In
Class

5

Here is a piece of graffiti seen regularly in college men's rooms (it might be in the women's rooms also; I didn't see it there):

I don't know whether or not these words were actually spoken by the gentlemen in question. Frankly, I never went to school with any of them. I'm quoting graffiti here, not history. It's trite but relevant.

The title of this chapter is: *Be In Class*. "Be In Class" sounds passive. At first glimpse, classes may seem like a passive thing. As you are well aware, there is much to be gained passively in class.

You still realize the value of reading ahead as the lecture reinforces the material. You will also spare yourself a good case of writer's cramp since your command of that material enables you to take fewer notes. After all, you've read ahead and you've stayed ahead. What more is there to do but lie back and soak up the reinforcement?

There's a lot more. Reread that graffiti. To be is to do! With RASABIC, being in class is an *active* thing. You *do* it.

You might ask why I didn't call this chapter "Do In Class."

Well, I thought about it, but I didn't like the acronym "RASADIC."

Just as you have more time at night because of your efficient studying, you will have more time in class. You are not consumed by a frenzy of note scribbling. What are you going to do with that time?

You are going to enter the active level in class. You are going to use that time to pay attention to the professor. And when I say pay attention to the professor, I am talking about a whole lot more than listening.

I'm talking about the things you will *do to* the professor. The subtle and not-so-subtle things that will influence the professor to give you a better grade.

If you stop reading right now and follow only that part of the RASABIC system with which you are now familiar, you stand a damn good chance of doing very well in college.

BUT, you would only be practicing academics as a science. In this chapter I begin your introduction to the *art* of being a student. Science can be very limiting in its preoccupation with boundaries. Art is about blurring and removing boundaries.

This chapter is about all the things you can do without a pencil and paper that have a direct bearing on your grade. Very few people will discuss these concepts with you. There are two reasons for this. Either they don't understand the concepts, or they do.

The principle of the subjective grade

Here is a quote from a guy who really knows how to set a tone:

> "All that we see or seem
> Is but a dream within a dream."
> *- Edgar Allan Poe*

I'm not going to pretend I know exactly what Poe meant by this. I was not a lit major. Here is what it means to RASABIC:

> "Perception is an extremely flexible
> and malleable commodity."

No one acts on reality. Everyone acts on perceptions.

Here's Mr. Stock Investor. He buys a stock when he perceives that the stock will go up. Sometimes the stock goes down.

When it does go down, the reality is he should not have bought the stock. But Mr. Stock Investor did by the stock. He acted on his perceptions, not on reality. Not only that, but he backed his perceptions with cold hard cash.

Mr. Stock Investor was committed to his perceptions and he acted upon them. That is what people do. We are each the genius of our own perspective.

People talk about reality, but they act on their perceptions. This is because most people treat their perceptions as reality. This gives them the illusion of confidence, enabling them to make big decisions where they lose lots of money.

This is not a big philosophy discussion. The point is: When you need something from someone else, the only reality that counts is that person's reality, which means their perceptions.

In the classroom you must deal with the professor's reality. That is the only one that counts. This should not make you feel helpless. This should make you happy and excited. Here's why:

You can influence perceptions.

It is a fact that the professor will give you your grade. That grade has little to do with the reality of your learning. That grade has only to do with the professor's perception of your learning. It is crucial to understand this difference. This difference is the essence of the *principle of the subjective grade*.

Your grade is based on the professor's perception of your knowledge, not on your actual knowledge. Anything you do that improves this perception will improve your grade.

Or, as Poe might have put it:

> "All in school that you score or grade,
> Is but an impression which you have made."

There were times when I received a higher grade than someone else who knew the material better than I did. It may be a character flaw on my part, but I did not go to the records office and attempt to correct the situation. After all, I had worked for my grade. I worked on getting the benefit of the professor's positive perception. The other student did not. I benefited through my application of the principle of the subjective grade.

The fact is that life is unfair. We are all familiar with this. If you have trouble with the idea of trying to tip the scales in your favor, you'd better stop reading. This chapter may be rather upsetting for you.

A word to the doubters

Some people deny the principle of the subjective grade. They say that grading is objective. Test scores determine the grade, not the professor's perception.

This is naive.

First ask yourself: Who grades the tests and papers?

The professor, usually. How do you think those test scores are formed? They are formed from the professor's perception of your answers.

A professor once told me: "I couldn't make out what you were saying on number 14, but I know you know the material, so I gave you credit."

The five points I received for that question gave me a 92 instead of an 87. That made the test grade an A instead of a B, which resulted in an A for the course. It was a final exam during my freshman year. I learned a valuable lesson that day.

The answer I gave was complete garbage. I did not know the correct answer. I did know, however, that I had created the perception in the professor's mind that I knew. I did that throughout the term. Without that groundwork, he would have graded the question exclusively on my answer and my GPA would have dropped.

RASABIC will ensure that you know most of the material, but it is unlikely that you will know everything every time. Sometimes you will draw a blank on a test.

Lot's of people tell you not to leave answers blank. RASABIC tells you how to create perceptions that create credit for the garbage you do put down.

Next ask yourself: Has a professor ever given a different grade than test scores would indicate?

The answer to this question is a conditional "yes."

Students occasionally get higher grades than their test scores indicate if the professor believes they know the material. That belief is a result of the professor's perception of the student. I have seen and experienced this many times.

Professors never give a grade lower than test scores indicate. If they do, they must defend it against a student complaint. That is very difficult to do without solid evidence of cheating.

Technically, they would have to defend a higher grade against a student complaint as well. Not surprisingly, those cases rarely come to trial.

Some people will tell you that in a 400-student lecture course, this stuff won't do you any good. It is true you will not have the opportunity to apply all these concepts in that scenario, but you'll still have some. In very large classes, you will rely primarily on your efficient study techniques. Techniques which you learned in the last two chapters.

It is also true that there aren't many large classes. As you get into higher level courses, the class size shrinks dramatically. The higher you go, the smaller the class. If you don't attend a very big school, you may never have any enormous classes. Any class with less than sixty or seventy students will give you complete freedom to apply all of these concepts.

Some students just don't want to believe in the principle of the subjective grade. By now, you should perceive its value. It is time to talk about what to do.

Professors

Professors are the focus of the classroom. They are *it*. Let's talk about them.

Professors are not the enemy. They are professionals doing a job. They are also people who seek the same things we all do: satisfaction, security, comfort, pleasure, and a feeling of significance.

However, because they are professors, the particular things they seek for their satisfaction and pleasure differ from ours.

Having taught at the high school, college, and business levels, I am acutely aware of what a class is like from both sides of the desk.

This section takes you inside the mind of the professor. By understanding how professors think and respond, you will understand more of the psychological dynamics of the classroom and how you will benefit.

The first thing to understand about professors is that they want you to win. They want you to learn and understand the material. They want to give you an A. They are on your side!

Why do you think they are professors? They have some love of the subject they teach, and they want to impart that feeling and knowledge to youthful, hungry minds like yours. This feeling exists in all professors, even the grumpy ones who won't admit it.

Professors must stand in front of the class and teach for the whole term. They are making a time investment. If they think no one learned anything, they feel as though they wasted their time and effort. No one enjoys that feeling.

On the other hand, if they gain the perception that everyone has learned everything, they feel great. Their time was worthwhile and well spent. They are wonder-prof, and they get a t-shirt with a big "W" on the chest!

Usually what happens is that some students learn the material and others do not. The students who do will give the professor a feeling of accomplishment, the perception of having touched another life. The professor senses their enthusiasm. This is very positive. When the professor thinks of these students, she gets a positive association, a nice feeling.

Suppose the professor is thinking of one of these good students because the student is on the borderline between an A and a B. What do you think happens? That's right, the good feeling turns into a good grade. An A!

The point is: You must generate the perception that you are impacted by the lectures and excited about learning the material.

Professors have less respect for a genius who gets a 90% than they do for an average learner who gets a 79%.

So what?

So this: The genius on the borderline is going to get knocked down. The average learner on the borderline is going to get bumped up.

Professors favor the underdog. That's another reason they teach! If your professor believes you are trying, you will get the benefit of the doubt. This benefit could be worth an extra .25 to .50 in GPA per term.

The point is: You must generate the perception that you are trying hard to learn the material, whether or not you actually are.

Do you know what lonely is? Lonely is standing in front of a room with fifty to ninety eyes all focused on you. Seeing the apprehension in their faces as they wait for you to imbue them with the knowledge they need to pass your course.

Teaching a class is a lonely business. That loneliness is very uncomfortable for professors. They never get used to it.

Do you know how to make a person feel good about you? Make 'em feel good. An anxious person will always develop an immediate and positive association with anyone he perceives as relieving his anxiety. Ask any comedian. Make people happier and they will like you.

The point is: Anything you can do to relieve the professor's loneliness and anxiety in class will come back to you, favorably, in your grade.

No matter how much a professor likes you, he must have some solid evidence on which to base a grade. Unless there is the clear perception you have learned some material, you will never get an A.

That evidence does not have to be test scores and papers. Professors are very willing to make excuses for you if they like you. They are ready to assume you don't test well, or perhaps you have trouble expressing yourself. If they perceive you as knowing something, they can grant amazing latitude in the way this knowledge is demonstrated.

If a professor is motivated, she can make a mountain out of a molehill, but at some point you must supply the molehill.

There are many opportunities to do this. Most of them occur in class.

The point is: You must generate the perception of some acquired knowledge during the course.

There you have it, simply put. A four-point program to achieve the highest subjective grade possible:

1. You must generate the perception that you are impacted by the lectures and excited about learning the material.
2. You must generate the perception that you are trying hard to learn the material, whether or not you actually are.
3. Anything you can do to relieve the professor's loneliness and anxiety in class will come back to you, favorably, in your grade.
4. You must generate the perception of some acquired knowledge during the course.

Now you know what to do. Let's talk about how to do it.

In-class behavior

Good in-class behavior has nothing to do with being polite and well mannered. Nor does it mean being rude.

Good in-class behavior means using goal directed behavior to get every possible grade advantage while in class. This is another place you will use your awareness.

There are many components to in-class behavior. I'll tell you what they are and how they work. Use your awareness. Recognize moments of opportunity in class. Start accumulating points on your subjective grade.

The lion's share of the meat in this section is concerned with implementing the four points outlined in the last section. We'll take them one at a time. Ready? Here we go.

You must generate the perception that you are impacted by the lectures and excited about learning the material.

Impact is change. If the professor is to see impact, the professor must perceive change.

How can the professor see me change without knowing who I am? Must I supply each professor with my life story in order to demonstrate the change?

No. You will supply the background at the same time you demonstrate the impact.

How will I do that?

Acting.

In films, it's called character development. You see stunning changes in film characters whom you have only known for an hour. That doesn't happen in real life, but who says classes are real life?

Classes are school life, and you are playing the role of the successful student. Here's some direction:

Regurgitation won't do it. Regurgitation proves you are at least a parrot, but no more.

You must take a concept and apply it. Relate what the professor said to something the professor didn't say. Applied knowledge indicates you have risen to the level of higher primate. College is not the parrot jungle. It's more like a barrel of monkeys.

The best place to apply knowledge is in your own life. As the professor lectures, ideas and images will spring to your mind. It happens frequently. You will hear about theories and studies that have been done. You will see these things occurring in your own life.

Don't keep it a secret. Let the professor know. Right then and there, during in-class discussion. Or, if that is uncomfortable for you, make a note and do it immediately after class. Go right up to the professor and explain how the lecture brought back a specific incident in your life with a fresh point of view.

You need three things: an incident, your former outlook, and your new, changed outlook brought on by the eye-opening insights you have just received. Real or fiction, show conviction.

Here are two examples from widely divergent subjects, Art History and Physics:

Art History Example

You have just heard a lecture about how technique and style are used to identify the artist:

"I realized something during your lecture that really struck me.

"I've always enjoyed handwriting analysis. I always thought the idea that everyone can be identified by their handwriting is really cool. It's like they put a part of themselves in every word they write, like tracks or footprints.

"During your lecture, I started to see how painters do the same thing with their paintings. You can see the artist in his work, just like you can see a person in their handwriting. It makes me think that everyone has a kind of signature to everything they do.

"It made me realize that I get the same kind of satisfaction from this course that I do from handwriting analysis. I knew I liked this, but now I can see why. Thank you."

Be prepared to look very interested as the professor expands on what you just said. How everyone does add a unique touch to everything they do, and how with practice, you too can develop a keen eye for style in anything. The professor might even mention that you are already on your way, and you are. To an A.

Physics Example

A few days after finishing a chapter on vectored force analysis:

"Excuse me sir, but I have to tell you that your course is really beginning to irritate me.

"I was walking across the quad yesterday and I saw a leaf get blown off a tree. I always used to like watching leaves float along with the wind.

"But now, as I'm watching this leaf, I'm seeing all these little arrows pointing out all the forces acting on it. There's a big arrow for gravity below it, and a whole bunch of other arrows around the edges. They're growing and shrinking with the gusts, pushing the leaf around with the vector sum. Always the vector sum.

"I can't remember what it was like to just sit and watch the leaf sail. You've ruined me, so I just wanted to say, thanks a lot."

Be sure to smile, emphasizing the sarcasm.

The professor will not say much to this one, but he will smile back. This is exactly what he went through when he studied. He will see himself in you. You have just scored some solid points.

This is called telling an impact story. All you are doing is relating an idea to the professor. It just so happens that the story reflects the impact the material has on you. Professors like the feeling of having had an impact upon you.

These examples are over-dramatized for the purpose of making the idea clear. You should be more subtle. It may seem silly, but it works.

Sometimes a lecture will not suggest any specific incident in your life, but it does inspire a fantasy of something you wish had happened.

Think about this fantasy for a while. Play it out in your mind and make it real. Then tell it as though it did happen. Why not?

Relax and be creative. I guarantee the professor will not do a background check to verify the authenticity of your story.

If you are uncomfortable about going up and talking after class, or if you don't have the time because of your next class, use office hours. Professors always have office hours, so you can see them out of class. Make a note of your idea, rehearse your story (not too much), then go and earn your Oscar.

You can even do it when you see your professor around campus. Don't take up too much time, but don't worry about taking some. If the professor believes you're interested, they're interested.

Do this one or two times during the term. If you are sincere, it will make a lasting impression in your favor.

You must generate the perception that you are trying hard to learn the material, whether or not you actually are.

How do you communicate hard work to the professor?

You could say: "Gee, I work really hard in your class. I am certainly a hard worker in this subject."

That sounds silly, doesn't it? The professor is more likely to wonder about you than respect you.

It is always better to show, rather than tell. A picture is worth a thousand words. Be demonstrative, and let people reach their own conclusions. People believe more strongly in their own observations than those pointed out by others.

"You must generate the perception that you are trying hard...

...whether or not you actually are."

You must do things that show the professor you are working hard, so he can see it for himself. The surest way to do this is by asking questions.

Questions are the most significant form of student-teacher communication. When a student asks a question, they not only ask something, they say something. Professors are keenly aware of the questions students ask. It is their only way, other than tests, of knowing what is in the minds of the students.

When you ask a question, you not only show what you don't know, you also show what you *do* know. Professors judge you every time you ask a question. They judge you on the level of the question. Here is an example:

Pretend you are the professor during an astronomy lecture. You have just finished explaining that the sky is blue because of the atmosphere, but did not discuss why. You are now taking questions:

"What color is the sky?" This student might as well stand up and shout, "Hi everybody. Don't mind me, I'm totally clue-less."

"Why is the sky blue?" This student is farther ahead than the first. His question shows he is past the color issue and is curious about a deeper level of detail that he missed in the lecture.

"How does the atmosphere make the sky blue?" This student's question shows that she has already surpassed the understanding of the other two. She is probing deeper still, beyond the scope of the lecture.

Professors hate to hear the first kind of question. It shows the student has learned nothing.

They expect the second kind, which confirms some knowledge, but not all that was presented.

The third kind of question makes a professor sit up and take note. Here is a student who understands what was said and still desires to understand more. This is the kind of student who makes teaching enjoyable. The professor will remember this student as one who works diligently and with comprehension.

You want to ask the third kind of question. This won't be difficult. You should already have some written down from your reading. Here is where you put them to good use.

There is an old saying: "It is wiser to keep your mouth shut and be thought a fool than to open it and remove all doubt." This is good advice, for fools.

You are not a fool. You know the material already from reading ahead. You do not ask stupid questions. Your questions demonstrate not only your work, but also your desire to move a little beyond.

When students ask no questions, the professor assumes they know nothing, not everything. They figure the students are lost and/or confused. You must ask questions to shield yourself from this presumption. Ask questions regularly.

Don't limit your questions to the classroom. Take your questions to a professor during office hours at least twice per term. You can mix them with your impact stories if you like.

The best questions leap farthest beyond the scope of in-class lecture. These are the questions to ask during office hours.

Here is a way to spend fifteen minutes and come up with a stunning question. It is called *Question Prospecting*.

Go to the library. Find the Library of Congress (or Dewey Decimal) number for your subject and go to the stacks. Peruse the shelves. Find titles that match the material you are familiar with or recognize from your reading. Grab one.

Flip through the book, reading occasional paragraphs. You will see familiar topics discussed in different ways, or topics that belong in the upper level version of your course. Rephrase this material into a question, or alter a question in the book. Know at least a little about the answer.

Take that question to your professor during office hours. Whether or not you are interested, sit through the answer with an interested look. Don't check your watch.

This question is not about asking. It is about showing. This question demonstrates how your interest and knowledge exceed the scope of the course. It shows you are doing more work than other students in the class.

Do not be surprised when you get a very positive reaction. If the professor suggests some additional reading for you, write it down! Next time you go prospecting, pick up that title and do it again.

The professor will wear your stimulation and interest with pride. That pride will show up in your grades.

Anything you can do to relieve the professor's loneliness and anxiety in class will come back to you, favorably, in your grade.

You recall from the last section that teaching is a lonely and anxious business. There are several things you will do to help alleviate this feeling for the professor.

The first and most important is eye contact. I cannot overemphasize the importance of eye contact, but I'll try.

When someone is speaking to you, they expect to see your eyes. Looking a speaker in the eyes gives him the feeling of being heard. It makes a speaker feel the listener is attentive, interested, and engaged. It gives the speaker a positive feeling about the listener.

If the listener avoids eye contact, negative stuff starts to happen. The listener is perceived as evasive, uncaring, and bored. The speaker is not happy, and they see the listener as the cause.

Try this: While a friend or acquaintance is talking to you, avoid his eyes. Don't look away, just stare at his nose or eyebrows as he speaks. Always keep your face toward him, but don't look into his eyes. Watch what happens.

A patient person will start to ask if you are hearing him. He will seek more acknowledgment for what he is saying. An impatient person will become irritated and aggressive. He will speak louder or with greater stress. He might even stop talking to you altogether.

In either case, you will see the speaker become progressively more uncomfortable as he talks to you. This is not a positive experience for him.

"Anything you can do to relieve the professor's loneliness and anxiety in class will come back to you, favorably, in your grade."

Next try this: Get together with all the students in one of your classes before the teacher arrives. Get everyone to avoid looking at the teacher during the class. Tell them this is a big psychology experiment. Do what the teacher says. Don't be disruptive. Simply avoid looking at the teacher.

This won't go on very long. I don't know if you have ever seen this done, but it is quite remarkable. In most cases, the teacher will become hostile within five minutes. You will hear the irritation in her voice as she becomes increasingly uncomfortable. Shortly after this, she'll blow up, assigning a lot of homework or suddenly declaring a pop quiz. This is a good time to call it off and explain the situation.

Professors and teachers need to feel acknowledged while teaching. The best way to do this is with eye contact. Whenever you are not writing or reading the board, look into the professor's eyes.

After a while you will notice that they seem to speak more to you than to the other students. This is because the professor will spend more time looking at you as he lectures to the class. This is because when he looks at you, he sees eyes looking right back. This makes him feel more comfortable and gives him a positive feeling.

He will associate this feeling with you. Thinking of you, while grading your paper perhaps, will give him a pleasant feeling. He will pass this on to you in your grade.

This happens subliminally. The professor is not explicitly aware of it. But it does happen, and you do benefit.

To paraphrase Svengali: "Look into their eyes."

The leading question is also a useful tool. Professors are like trails in the forest; they are always leading somewhere.

You have read ahead and you will frequently know where the professor is leading before it is obvious to the rest of the class. Ask a question that leads directly to the destination.

When you hear, "I was just getting to that," or "Good question, let's talk about that now," you should smile. You just made it clear that the lecture is having the desired effect, at least in your case. This will make the professor aware that she is reaching someone. This is positive reinforcement, and it will be appreciated.

Don't overdo it. Use the leading question sparingly. It will serve you well.

Another way to put the professor at ease is to participate actively in class. Jump into discussions. Don't hesitate to answer questions. Be a student on whom the professor can rely for a reasonable response. A demonstration that she is not teaching to the air. Proof that the material is learnable.

The pregnant pause after asking a question of the class is the most uncomfortable time for a professor. Don't let it hang too long. Be the class contraceptive by breaking up these awkward moments.

You must generate the perception of some acquired knowledge during the course.

Hey, it's not all psychodrama. The easiest way to demonstrate knowledge it to have knowledge. By reading ahead and digesting the material, you will have an enormous pool of knowledge on which to draw. The key is to make the professor, and everyone else, see it!

Just as questions are the way to demonstrate hard work, answers are the way to show that work is paying off. Answer questions frequently. Speak out. Get involved in discussions.

Active participation is more than a way to relax the professor. It is the primary method for demonstrating what you know. It's also fun.

Believe me, if you do your reading you will know the answers to most questions in class. Get your hand up every time you do. Don't be shy.

After a while the professor will not call on you anymore. This is good. It means he is sure you know the answer and he would like to hear from someone else. Sometimes you may even hear the magic words: "We know you know it; let's give the others a chance." Translation: "You're getting an A. Relax."

This is how I was able to get credit for garbage answers. Professors were so sure I knew the material that they tended not to believe it when I was off base, and they gave me credit.

When you do answer questions, don't be cocky. Answer with a touch of doubt in your voice, then appear pleased to find you are correct.

By the second half of the term, you are established as an answer machine. Back off a little. Don't raise your hand right away for a question. If no one else attempts to respond after five or ten seconds, raise your hand slowly if you know the answer.

This does two things. It reminds the teacher that you still have the answers, and it intimidates the class when you are right.

Don't knock it, intimidation is worth points in your GPA. If the class is aware of at least one person who knows the answers, it puts more pressure on the rest. Flustered students make mistakes, which reduces the curve and makes any score you get seem better.

This may sound ugly, but it's true.

The herd lives by the curve. They worry about someone pushing it up. In my senior year, when I would walk into the first day of a course, I would actually hear a groan from the other students.

"There goes the curve," they'd say. They were right, and it scared them.

The only people who didn't groan were other good students. They were never intimidated. When you know the material, you have nothing to worry about.

Correcting the professor

Professors are human beings and they make mistakes. They rarely make big ones, but they do make mistakes.

When they do, it's an opportunity for you. Seeing and correcting these oversights will remove any possible doubt a professor may have about your thorough understanding of everything going on in class.

Don't be reticent or scared to correct the professor, but do be very tactful. There is no need, or call, to be obnoxious or insulting.

If you are courteous, professors will not take a correction as being shown up. They don't want to put mistakes on the board. If they miswrite something on the board, and everyone copies misinformation into their notes, there will be big trouble on the next exam. Everyone will have the wrong answer and they will blame the professor for that mistake. Professors are aware of this and they would prefer to avoid it, believe me. They will appreciate your correction, if done properly. Here is how to do it properly:

First let the professor continue for a minute, to see if he picks it up and corrects it on his own.

If not, raise your hand and get his attention. When called upon, ask if the point in question is correct.

Don't say, "That's wrong."

You should ask in a soft tone, "I'm not sure I understand that last part (point it out). Could you please explain it?"

On second glance, he will usually see the mistake and correct it. Good professors will make a funny joke at this point.

Sometimes you will be wrong and have the point cleared up for you. That's great. You learned something and never accused the professor of being incorrect.

Once in a great while you may see something that you know is wrong, and the professor can't see it. He will continue to present it as being true.

At this point, state what you think it should be. If the professor continues to maintain that it is correct, DO NOT ARGUE. Do not create a confrontation. Just shut up at this point and let it drop.

It is fine to correct a professor, but you should never confront or embarrass one in class. That would affect your subjective grade in a very negative way.

The professor knows you are a solid student. He will review the material after class, find the mistake, and correct it during the next lecture. He will have no ill feeling toward you. He will admire your awareness and grace.

I was in an upper level economics class when the professor was doing a graphical analysis of a point in fiscal theory.

She drew something on the graph that was just plain wrong. It had nothing to do with economics. It was geometrically impossible. It couldn't be right.

I raised my hand and asked if the graph was correct. She said it was. I explained that there appeared to be a geometric contradiction in the picture.

She focused on the principle involved. I said that my concern was not about the economic theory, but rather the geometric representation. It was literally impossible the way it was drawn.

The class was very conscious of this interaction by now, and I could see she was sticking to her position, which I knew was incorrect.

I could have gone up to the board and used some basic geometry to prove my point, but I didn't. I shut up and let the lecture continue. I refused to confront her on the point. No one else in the class seemed to see it either. If they did, they weren't talking.

Two days later, as I approached the classroom for the next lecture, she stopped me outside the class. She told me she had checked out her analysis with some other professors after the previous class and realized I was right.

We thanked each other, then I went into class and took my seat. I had always respected her tremendously, and my respect for her only grew.

At the beginning of this lecture, she announced that Mr. Warshaw had been correct in the last lecture, and re-drew the graph appropriately. Then she specifically thanked me in front of the whole class. She was making it clear that she approved of the correction.

I would never have mentioned our hallway conversation to anyone, but she did. It was important to her that the right information got out. She, like most professors do, showed real class in class.

She gave me an A and a real lift.

To illustrate a bad approach, I should tell you about another episode. There was one time when I did specifically embarrass a teacher with corrections. I was wrong in doing it, but I did it.

I was taking an upper level math course, and the professor was a graduate student I knew from other classes. His sole goal in life was to get his notes on the board. He had fifty minutes to get his teaching plan up there and, by God, he was going to do it.

He didn't like taking questions because they slowed his pace. He was more interested in getting his notes on the board than he was in having the students understand what he was teaching. Call me self-righteous, but this irritated the hell out of me. It was during a lecture near the end of the term that I got fed up with this attitude. I lost control and went for his tutorial throat.

We were in a small classroom on the fourth floor of an old building. There was a big open window on the left and a hallway door on the right. He was in the middle, scribbling his notes and not taking questions. There were only ten minutes left in the period and he was behind. Then he miswrote a calculation in the middle of a proof.

"Excuse me," I said, "but isn't that derivative incorrect?"

He half turned to me as he kept chalking the board furiously and muttered, "There's only a few minutes left; let me finish this proof. I don't want to get behind the other sections."

The other sections were being taught by his mentor and idol. He couldn't bear the thought of being perceived as a laggard. I decided it was time to be a jerk and I wouldn't give him a break.

"Excuse me, but how can you expect us to consider your derivation when it's based on a false premise?"

"OH! Very well," he grumbled, unable to argue the point. Quickly, he ran over to the equation in question and changed it. "There," he said with disdain, and lumbered over to where he had left off. "Let's continue."

His corrected answer was also wrong.

"Excuse me," I interrupted again, "but it's still wrong."

"We're running out of time. Can't you wait until this is done?" he asked, beginning to lose his composure.

"It's not done if it's not correct, is it?" I asked, not really believing I was saying this, but enjoying it nonetheless. He and I had never been particularly close.

"Ooooooooooh, FINE!" He was getting hot now. He stomped over and changed the answer once again.

I couldn't believe it, but it was still wrong! I couldn't stop now.

"Excuse me," I said, nearly giggling at his point, "That still isn't right."

Now he was really pissed. He was extremely anal-retentive and didn't like losing control. He was uncomfortably close to the edge right now.

Without saying a word, he stormed over to the desk in the middle of the classroom. In an effort to recompose himself, he picked up all his notes for the entire term, planning to straighten and align them on the table surface. Squaring up a stack of paper is good therapy for the compulsively orderly.

As fate would have it, when he brought the stack down he missed the edge of the desk. One hundred twenty five pages of notes scattered themselves randomly across the floor in front of the classroom.

That was it. His face bloomed into the most amazing shade of purple I have ever seen. He glared at me briefly, then he looked over at the window. For a moment, I really thought he was going to jump. Instead he turned the other way and steamed out the door. Class was dismissed for the day.

Nothing was ever said about the incident. Everyone just let it drop, so to speak.

He gave me an A in the course. He explained how he had tried not to, but he couldn't avoid it. I was among the highest scores in all the sections of the course. Remember, it is easier to give a higher grade than a lower grade.

Although this worked out okay, this is a glaring example of what not to do. I never even came close to doing this at any other time in my entire education. I acted like a jerk. As weird and amusing as it may have been, I still regret it today. Even with the rationalizations I use in the story, it was inexcusable. Sorry Dave.

Correcting mistakes will make a valuable contribution to your subjective grade. Don't be afraid to do it. Just remember how to do it right.

Always treat professors with dignity and respect, especially when correcting mistakes. Never confront them. Never argue with them. Never say the words, "You are wrong."

One other thing. Never take a class from a grad student with whom you have a known personality conflict.

The benefit of the benefit of the doubt

If you get 100% on everything you touch, you will get an A. If you honestly strive to achieve this goal, you will almost surely get an A. If you rely on achieving this goal, you will be a fool.

You will not miss much, but you will miss here and there. In some subjects, you may never miss a point. That never happened to me.

No matter what happens, a solid A is an A. However, you may not always be solid. RASABIC can ensure you never worry about a C, but nothing can guarantee a solid A every time. There will be borderline cases. The borderline is always resolved by the subjective grade.

Another name for the subjective grade is "the benefit of the doubt." The techniques you have been reading are all about getting the benefit of the doubt. They make sure any questions about your answers, your papers, or your grades are resolved in your favor.

Here is what that means: Suppose you take thirty-five courses for your degree. Suppose further that eleven of those courses wind up on the borderline.

The difference between those decisions going for you or against you is .3 GPA points. That means nothing when comparing a 2.1 with a 2.4 GPA, but the difference between a 3.3 and a 3.6 could be the difference between graduating with honors or graduating without distinction. That could be the difference between a good job or no job.

When employers come to interview at a college, they rarely walk in and say, "We'd like to talk to your average students, please." They are looking for distinguished students. Wouldn't you?

These people don't know anything about you, except what they have on the sheet in front of them. The first thing they look at is your GPA, and they compare it with those of the other applicants. Numbers are the easiest thing to compare. Bigger numbers impress them.

It pays to be impressive.

This is the benefit of the benefit of the doubt.

Getting test questions

You can get most of the test questions in advance, in class. Professors give them out all the time.

So why doesn't everybody get an A?

Because they don't pay attention.

Once in a while, a professor will say, "I'd write this down because this will definitely be on the test." He isn't kidding. You should, of course, write it down and study it for the next test.

This is called *cueing* a question. This is the most obvious form of cueing a question. Professors cue almost all of their test questions, but they are rarely this overt about it. You must learn to read the professor more effectively to get the questions you seek.

First examine the verbal cues. There are many things that professors say to indicate the current topic will be a test question. Here are a few:

"What all this means is . . ."
"The point of this analysis is . . ."
"We must realize that . . ."
"You should see that . . ."
"Clearly, this shows . . ."
". . . Is this absolutely clear?"
". . . Does everyone follow this?"
". . . Is everyone with me?"
"Stop me right now if you don't see this."

Anytime you hear any one of these catch phrases, make a note of what the professor is referring to and put a big "T" next to it. Especially: "Stop me right now if you don't see this." It's like a neon sign.

There are two behavioral cues to look for as well.

Whenever a professor stops the lecture for a moment to flip through his book or his notes, there is a very high probability that the next thing you hear will be on the next test. Write it in your notebook and mark it with a "T."

When professors review, they are checking for important points they haven't covered yet. The biggest one they see is likely to be the next thing they present. This isn't perfect, but it has a very high success rate.

The other cue occurs when a professor stops to get the attention of a student who is talking to a neighbor or drifting off. If you ever hear a professor say something like: "Mr. Procrastantine. Are you with us?" or "Perhaps Slag would like to share his insight with the rest of the class," get ready for a test question. Note the next thing presented and give it a "T."

There is rarely a moment when everyone in the class is paying attention. The only time professors make an effort to get attention is when they are about to present something they feel is very important. Something they will put on a test.

If a professor ever gives a pop quiz and then complains to the class about the results of that quiz, those questions will definitely be on the next exam. Guaranteed.

Very few professors will use a test question that was not specifically covered in class. The only exceptions are from outside reading assignments, and even then it is rare. It is almost an unwritten law. This is another reason that being in class is so important.

They will be cueing their questions. They can't help it. Know how to read your teachers, then mark the questions.

Before each exam, review everything you marked in your notes with a "T." See how many of these actually appear on the test. You will be pleasantly surprised.

Review the questions you didn't have marked with a "T." Try to remember the classes in which that material was covered. Did the professor do anything unusual when covering this point? If so, you have discovered another cue. Every professor has her own cues. Learn them and use them.

Tests are much easier when you know the questions.

Pop quizzes

Review your notes before class. Allow yourself two minutes.

If you're practicing what RASABIC is preaching, pop quizzes are jokes for which you get credit. Really, you'll be laughing all the way to the Dean's list.

Classroom geography

Everyone tells you to sit up front. Studies have been done which show that students who sit up front and attend every class tend to get better grades. Duh. That's the same as saying living people tend to breathe. What they don't tell you is that no one ever gets a good grade *because* they sit up front.

Better students sit up front because they are told to sit up front. They get good grades because they study, attend classes, and do the work necessary to succeed in school. They do more work than I did. They also don't mind sitting up front.

Bad students are afraid to sit up front. It is intimidating to be near the teacher when you don't know what's going on. It feels bad, so they avoid it. It's just common sense.

As far as the professor's attention is concerned, consider five students seated as follows in a classroom: one in front, one in back, one on the extreme right center, one on the extreme left center, and one in the middle. Which student gets the most attention? Which student gets the least attention?

If you answered with any of the five students mentioned, you missed it.

The student who gets the most attention is the one who attracts the most attention. The student who gets the least attention is the one whom the professor feels doesn't need attention.

Where you sit doesn't have much bearing on your grade. What you do while sitting there makes a big difference. Choose your seat for good reasons, not for clichés.

RASABIC says to sit at or near the front. Here are three specific advantages to sitting near the head of the class:

➼ You can see the instructor and what she's doing without interference.

➼ You can use eye contact easily.

➼ You are right in the professor's face with your hand up, and the class can see it too.

All of these things will help you implement RASABIC. You don't have to be in the front row, just be near the front with a clear, unobstructed view.

If you think you would be better off in another seat, take that seat. There is rarely assigned seating in college, so don't treat it that way.

Don't forget, it's what you do that counts, not where you do it.

A brief word on the first class

Before plowing into the course work proper, most professors will begin the first class meeting by laying out the structure of the course.

They will tell you what material they intend to cover and the composition of your grade. Here is what you want to do:

Get the syllabus

A *syllabus* is a course outline. It should state what material will be covered and when. It may also have due dates for tests and papers. In short, it lays out the course for you.

If one is available, get it! If not, ask enough questions to make your own. Ask about tests and papers. Ask what chapters of the text will and won't be covered. If there is anything you want to know, ask.

Get the grade composition

How many tests will there be? How much will each test count? What will they cover? Are there any papers due? Does homework count toward your grade? Is there extra credit available? What about pop quizzes?

Find out everything the professor will use to determine your grade. Find out how much each part counts.

Each professor is unique. Some will give only a midterm and final, each worth 50%. Some professors will have many small assignments totaling 40% of your grade, and a comprehensive final for 60%.

Is the final comprehensive? A comprehensive final covers the entire course. Or will it only cover the material presented since the last test? Will tests be graded straight up or with a curve? Find out.

Professors usually give a breakdown of your grade. They will tell you about each assignment and test, and how much it counts. If they don't tell you, ask.

Get the reading list

A *reading list* is a list of the books and articles that you are expected to read during the course. Not often, but once in a while, professors will put questions on tests that were never covered in class. They are covered in the outside reading.

If there is a reading list, get it! Then read as much as you can, as soon as you can. Ask the professor which items on the reading list are required for which tests and projects.

If no reading list is presented, ask if one exists.

Get the office hours

Office hours are the time and place you may meet with the professor out of class. Get the time and the place.

Do you know what to do if the professor doesn't give this information right away? That's right. Ask.

There is a common thread running through this section: Asking questions. The point of the first day of class is not only to start the course lectures, it is also to find out as much as you can about the course itself. Ask all the questions you want until you feel you have all the information you need.

Get the syllabus, get the grade composition, get the reading list, get the office hours, and then get on with the course work.

Ask about anything you want to know. Never be afraid to ask questions about a course. Questions are the only reason for having a professor in a course.

If you understand most of what you've read so far, you are certainly capable of a 3.7 GPA or better. If you don't, read it again. You're playing with your future.

From now on, we will refine your talents as a student and open up some other possibilities.

For those of you who just walked in

☆ Being In Class is not passive. It's active.

☆ Remember the Principle Of The Subjective Grade.

☆ People act on perceptions. Those perceptions can be influenced.

☆ Working on the professor's perception of you *is* working on your grade.

☆ You must generate the perception that you are impacted by the lectures and excited about learning the material.

☆ You must generate the perception that you are trying hard to learn the material, whether or not you actually are.

☆ Anything you can do to relieve the professor's loneliness and anxiety in class will come back to you, favorably, in your grade.

☆ You must generate the perception of some acquired knowledge during the course.

☆ Tell impact stories.

☆ Ask questions that indicate you are working.

☆ Go prospecting for questions.

☆ Make good eye contact in class.

☆ Don't be shy. Participate aggressively in class.

☆ Correct the professor. Tactfully!

☆ Get the benefit of the doubt.

☆ Learn to predict questions.

☆ Detect your professor's cues for test questions.

☆ Sit where you want, but have good reasons for sitting there.

☆ Get the syllabus, grade composition, reading list, and office hours on the first day of class.

☆ Ask questions. Find out what you need to know.

Studying

6

Studying is the cornerstone of a solid college program. If you do not study, you will not succeed in college. It's that simple.

This chapter is about studying. Not the mechanics of studying, but the goals and objectives of studying. Details are for children who cannot think for themselves. You are an adult.

Adults are given objectives and responsibilities, and they are expected to carry them out. This is how you are treated in college and in this book.

I would not presume to tell you exactly how to study, and I am highly suspicious of those who do. Studying is very personal. There are no fixed rules for how to study. Only you can know how *you* study most effectively.

This chapter includes some techniques and important considerations for studying. You will find them quite useful.

This chapter also explains what studying can accomplish. The upcoming sections on trees and methodology are not cookbook recipe stuff. They present the theory of how to *master* a subject, as opposed to merely acing it. These are things you might not need but should be aware of. It is up to you, with your own discipline and awareness, to achieve these results if you desire.

This may seem rather abstract, but if you can understand it you will be capable of mastering one of the real highlights of this book: How to get credit for garbage answers. That's coming up in the next chapter, but the best way to do it is explained in this one.

No other part of this book is as esoteric as this chapter, but some of your college courses will be. You might as well start practicing now.

"Studying is very personal...

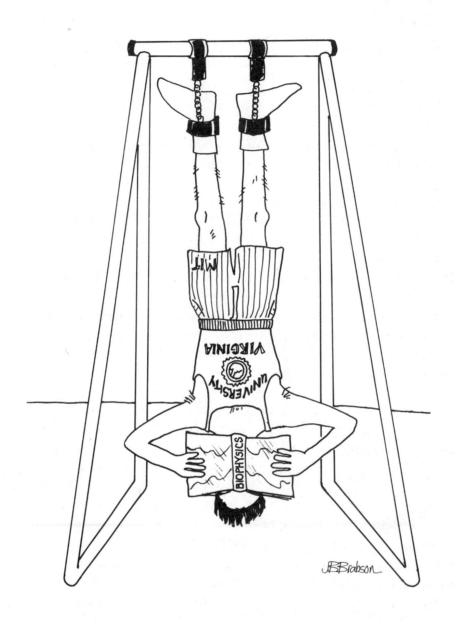

...only you can know how you study most effectively."

What are you doing?

Studying has no direct impact on your grade.

What?

That's right. Studying has no direct impact on your grade.

Tests, papers, homework, and class time are the only things that have a direct impact on your grade.

Studying does, however, enable these things to have a positive impact on your grade.

Submitted for your perusal: An Olympic athlete about to compete in the men's 100 meter dash. All the events of his life mean nothing now. The only thing that matters is his performance during the medal race. Since this is the only time that counts, do you think he ever did anything about it before this moment?

Of course he did. He practiced. He prepared himself for this moment by devoting the majority of his life to making himself the best 100 meter dasher he could be.

If he never practiced running and still won the race, would he get the gold medal? Absolutely. The practice time he spent has no direct impact on the result of the race. Only his performance during the race is important.

Has any Olympic athlete ever won without practicing? No.

Practice is necessary to develop the ability to perform well at the critical moment. By improving the ability to perform, practice contributes indirectly.

Have other athletes practiced a lot and still lost? Sure, all but the winner. Practice cannot guarantee victory, but not practicing will guarantee failure.

Studying will enable you to answer questions, catch mistakes, and contribute insights that make you stand out in class. It will enable you to succeed in college.

Studying for college courses is like practicing for the Olympics, or building a strong foundation for a house, or sharpening your broadsword for a medieval battle. It can't guarantee success, but if you don't do it, you don't stand a chance.

Where to study

There are a multitude of study places in college. I will not attempt to tell you which are right. Some people need to study in a soundproof booth, others can't concentrate without a constant ninety decibel roar.

I give you the characteristics of a good study place. Choose a place that satisfies these criteria and your personal taste.

Here are three properties of a good study place:

➤ Reliably isolated
➤ Resource accessibility
➤ Concentration compatibility

Reliably isolated does not mean a mountain top in Tibet. It simply means you can count on not being interrupted. It is fine to be around lots of people, but they must be people who won't disturb you. Studying is not a team sport. There may be a substantial time penalty for violation of this principle.

Study groups are recommended by many people. I never found them useful. This does not mean they are bad; they simply did not suit my study style.

If you want to use a study group, that's fine too. Just be sure of one thing: Be sure you are not the smartest or best prepared person in the group. If you are a much better student than anyone else in the group, it is possible that you are not getting nearly as much benefit as the others.

A study group should be of mutual benefit for all and it should be tightly focused on the subject matter. Bull sessions or leeching sessions will never help you study.

Resource accessibility means you have, or are near, everything you need to do your work. You don't need to be in the library, but you must have all the books and materials necessary. That includes people.

Study near people who can help you with questions. When you do ask them, be courteous and don't linger after the answer. It is rude to stay and chat. Thank them and leave.

Concentration compatibility exists in a place where you can concentrate. A place where you can ask yourself questions and hear the answers. This has nothing to do with noise or activity level. Some people can study well at a football game. Others need a sensory deprivation tank. Suit yourself. Just be sure the suit fits.

A good study place has all three: it's reliably isolated, it has resource accessibility, and it has concentration compatibility. A good study place also has one other important characteristic: you feel comfortable there. Take a walk around campus and find several places that suit your needs.

Consider time of day as well. You might choose different places depending on when you study. Consider morning, afternoon, evening, night, and late night. When you have found two or three places for each study time, you're ready to roll.

Answers grow on trees

Most students think the result of effective study is knowing all the facts covered in the course. Consequently, they study by trying to memorize all the facts. These students must love working because they are taking the hardest and most painful route to success. The focus of study is not memorization; it's learning.

Memory is for knowing. Learning is for thinking. High school is about knowing. College is about thinking.

Thinking is more powerful than knowing. Here is an example:

Do you know every word in the dictionary? Probably not. Did you learn how to find every word in the dictionary? Yes.

It takes a long time to *know* all the words in the dictionary, and when you do, it takes a tremendous amount of effort to maintain that knowledge. On the other hand, *using* a dictionary is a simple process that is easy to learn and retain.

You don't know the dictionary, but you learned how to use the dictionary. By virtue of that learning, you have access to every word in the dictionary.

This is the nature of information. Everyone can choose between knowing all the facts or learning how to access the facts. Dictionaries, telephone books, and encyclopedias are based on this principle. Either memorize the information or learn how to find it. Obviously, we choose the latter. Few of us try to memorize the phone book. We see how that would be ridiculous.

Yet students still try to memorize facts for tests, rather than learn how these facts are accessed. I studied that way, until I found the tree of knowledge.

The *tree of knowledge* is a metaphor for a subject. Picture a tall tree in full bloom. There is a root system, a large trunk, several significant branches, and thousands of leaves. This tree represents all the information contained in the course.

The leaves are the facts, the final conclusions and observations of the subject. The trunk and branches are the organization of the facts, the ideas and theories on which these facts are based. The roots are the lingo of the course, the vocabulary and terms unique to the subject.

Like the tree, the subject wasn't always there. It grew over time to become the field of study it is today.

Subjects grow just like trees. They start with a few ideas and some new terminology (a sapling). The nutrient for the subject is intellectual attention. As great minds work on it, the subject grows.

The original ideas become strengthened into larger theories and postulates (the trunk and branches). The vocabulary also increases to facilitate theoretical discussion and growth (the root system becomes expansive).

Eventually, the theoretical work spawns observations and conclusions which validate the field of study (the leaves appear). In college, useful knowledge (a test answer) doesn't just show up. It is derived from a theoretical base and some terminology.

Most students try to memorize all the leaves on the tree. They don't understand that every leaf is a direct product of the roots and branches leading to it.

The RASABIC approach is to learn the roots and branches. If you know the vocabulary roots and theoretical branches, you can reach any factual leaf quickly. You will have a deeper, more fundamental understanding of the subject, and you will do so by memorizing less material (there are far fewer roots and branches than there are leaves).

For the RASABIC student, answers do grow on trees.

"The tree of knowledge...
represents all the information contained in a course."

Methodology

Every subject has its own style, its own special perspective, its own approach to solving problems. This approach dominates the thinking of people in the field. This approach is called the *Methodology* of the subject. Learning methodology is the ultimate goal of studying.

As you go on to higher level courses in a subject, you will find that the facts differ, but the methodology remains chiefly the same. The things you talk about change, but the *way* you talk about them remains the same. Methodology is the way things are talked about or approached in a subject.

Learn the methodology of a subject once and you will know it for all the courses. By studying this way the courses become easier as you progress, not harder.

Here is an equation that summarizes the tree model of learning (yes, I really did have a math major):

$$facts = lingo + organization$$

An equation means that both sides are the same, and that is true in this case as well. You can either memorize all the facts or you can learn the lingo, the organization, and how they are combined to create the facts. There is much less work and far greater benefit in learning the right side of this equation.

Wait a minute. I said to learn the methodology of the course, and methodology doesn't appear anywhere in the equation.

Ah, but it is there. Methodology is the way lingo and organization are combined to form the facts. Methodology is the "+" in the equation.

You will not find methodology in the answers; methodology is in the explanations. In a textbook, you find facts at the end of paragraphs. The methodology is contained in the bodies of those paragraphs. This is why you must concentrate when you study, and use your awareness.

The secret to efficient studying lies in understanding not only what is being said, but also *how* it is being said. What is the thinking that leads to a conclusion? This thinking is the methodology. Methodology is why a subject's tree of knowledge grew the way it did. Methodology is the subject's DNA.

How can I find the methodology?

As you read your textbook and listen to lectures, focus on the explanations. You will find, after a while, that the explanations start to sound the same. Even though the topics and questions are different, the approaches to the answers have a similar thread. That thread is the methodology.

Note this similarity and study it. Get to know the way answers are derived in your course. The simplest example is arithmetic:

When you learn multiplication, you are given a series of problems to work out. Each problem is different, having different numbers, but the process is the same. The methodology of multiplication is always the same.

You don't learn the product of every possible combination of numbers (the leaves of the tree). Instead, you learn the basic one-digit tables (the roots and branches) and you learn how to multiply larger numbers in general (the methodology). By combining these two things you can recreate the product of any combination of numbers.

You can do the same in all your courses. It just isn't as obvious as in arithmetic. You must study carefully to uncover the simpler approach.

When you uncover the methodology, you will find it easy to know most of the answers to test questions.

When you don't know an answer, methodology is invaluable for creating garbage answers that get full credit, as you'll see in the next chapter.

The study process

By understanding the tree of knowledge and methodology, your study process comes down to three steps:

1. Learn the lingo.
2. Examine the explanations carefully.
3. Extract and understand the methodology.

Do this in each course. Your study time will be minimal and your grades will be maximal.

Lists

That last section is very general. It is the methodology of studying. You may want a more solid picture of how to study while you get used to grasping methodology in the course work.

That's fine, here you are: Lists.

Whenever you finish a chapter in a textbook, make a list. Go back through the text and write down a one-sentence description of each important point in the chapter. Number each sentence.

Now review your list. Start with number one. Read that sentence to yourself. Now explain how that point was derived in the text. Answer these three questions for each point:

What are the premises and assumptions?
What problem does this point address?
How was this point arrived at?

You will not know everything the first time through. That's perfectly normal. Go back and find the answer. Think it through. Be able to answer each of the three questions for each sentence on your list.

When you know all the answers, hide the list. Take out a blank piece of paper and try to reconstruct the list. You know how many items there are because you numbered the points. See how many you can remember.

You will find an interesting phenomenon. Sometimes you won't remember the point, but you will remember the explanation for the point. Thinking about the explanation will lead you to the point. Congratulations. You are beginning to apply methodology.

Whenever you are standing in line for something (this will happen frequently), try to recreate some of your lists in your mind. It won't take long to completely internalize many lists. You're getting it. Review occasionally, and keep working on more lists.

Lists, lists, lists. Your brain has the capacity to hold more lists than you would like to think about. You won't overflow. It will actually become fun to play in your mind.

As you reconstruct the lists, the explanations will start to become clearer than the points. You are training yourself to find and use the methodology.

You will also find that one or two items are consistently missing from your reconstructed list. Get the original list and highlight these points. These are your trouble points. When it comes time to study for an exam, you will know exactly where to concentrate.

Read carefully and make your lists. Would you rather study from a few sheets of note paper or a hundred pages of text?

Do that again

OK. This chapter is about studying. You already know about reading ahead and staying ahead, which will take care of most of your factual needs. You know how you study best. I can't tell you how to do that.

This chapter is about the theory of studying. The big picture. The whole that is greater than the sum of the parts.

Every subject is a tree of knowledge. Learn the roots and branches. Study the terminology. Use the terminology to talk about the course. Study the explanations as well as the facts. The explanations are the substance of the subject. Facts are fluff.

By studying the explanations, you can learn the methodology of the subject. The methodology is the glue that holds the whole subject together. Methodology is the way scholars think in a subject.

Every textbook is full of it (you may have said this yourself at times). Textbooks are written to illustrate the methodology of a subject.

Learn the vocabulary. Learn and study the explanations. Get a feel for the methodology in the subject. When you have done this, you will astound anyone who questions you on the subject. It's not that difficult.

Lists are a valuable aid for studying in general and for learning methodology in particular. Make lists. Understand them. Then try to reproduce them mentally. You will know all your course work cold.

When the mundane becomes too fascinating

"Gee, look at that fly. Circle after circle after circle. Doesn't he ever get dizzy? I'll bet he doesn't have a test next week. Probably doesn't even have a student ID. Will he land on the red book or the green one? Definitely the green one. Come on, go for it. Get that green book."

When you catch yourself in this internal monologue—and you will—it is time for a break.

Get up and move around. Get your blood going. Studying is hard work. Concentrating is very draining. Physically draining!

Have a soda or a snack. Do it fast. Don't linger on breaks, but take them regularly. Think of what you will do with your free time later that night.

Occasionally you're simply not into it. No matter how hard you discipline yourself, you just don't feel like studying. Here is what you should do: Give up.

You're studied out, depleted. Don't fight yourself. Sitting in front of a book and feeling badly is a waste of time.

If you have been applying yourself, you should already have some cushion in your study time. Why not use it now? Don't feel badly about not studying. Allow yourself to be "off" now and then. Forgiveness is very important for a high achiever.

Besides, if you have been working diligently, you have earned the right to an occasional indulgence. Go out and do something fun, something spontaneous. If you aren't studying, you should be enjoying yourself.

Say good-bye to the fly and go grab some real entertainment.

Of course, if you are never into studying and are rarely putting in serious study time, forgiveness is not the answer. You are not studied out. You are screwing around.

Tests 7

If you are applying the RASABIC concepts consistently, you are already in the 90% range. Be confident. You know the material.

This chapter has some helpful tips on how to close that final gap between 90% and 100%.

Confrontation

A test is a confrontation between you and the professor on the field of knowledge. It is not a battle. There is no bad feeling on the professor's side of the field. Both of you want your test grade to be high.

The people who hate tests are the unprepared, the Slags. Many students live in a world of denial. They can't face the fact that college is about studying and getting grades. So they don't.

They run around and have "fun" all the time. The only time they are miserable is immediately before and during tests. This is the one time they must face the fact that they are wasting their college careers.

There is one other time they are miserable. When looking for a job after college.

By studying ahead and applying the concepts in Chapter 5, "Be In Class," you have prepared both yourself and the professor to deliver a high grade. The presumption is in your favor. Now it's time to cash in.

"A test is a confrontation between you and the professor on the field of knowledge."

You are prepared. You have done your work both in class and out. All you have to do is be yourself. You are a star student. You are a collegiate conquistador. Don't get nervous. The only thing that can stop you is a psychotic episode. That won't happen.

Feel the confidence you have earned. Relax and enjoy it. Taking a test is fun when you know your stuff, and you do.

Test preparation

You have already done it. RASABIC students don't study for tests, they review. Go back over your notes. Reread all the highlighted material in your text for this exam. Read it slowly and think it through.

Review your lists. Pay particular attention to the items that were your trouble points. Stick to the ideas you had questions about during the past weeks. You noted those questions and the answers; use them now. It is redundant to focus on what you already know. Concentrate on the things with which you have trouble.

Next, search back through your notes and find all the points you marked with a big "T." These are your probable test questions. Rehearse answering questions about these points. You will be giving most of these answers soon.

Take plenty of pens, pencils, and paper to a test. Take your books and notes; it might be an open book test. Resources should never be an issue during an exam.

Lastly, relax and get a good night's sleep. I once read a story in which the main character said: "Sleep is a weapon." This is true. Make sure it's in your arsenal.

Taking the test

Read the entire test first! You never know exactly what you will find.

Sometimes at the end of a test, you will find: "Answer only four of the nine questions. Answer in great detail." You don't want to see this after answering eight questions briefly. This is a dirty trick to be sure, but it doesn't matter if you read the test first.

When reading a test, scan for directions first. You must know how to take the test before attempting to do it. Don't ever get caught as in that last example. Especially if the professor says: "Read the test first," while handing it out. Professors never joke about instructions during a test.

Now review the questions. Read each question carefully. See if a definite answer pops into your head. Don't stick with questions on first reading. This is merely a quick assessment of the exam. If a question is not immediately obvious, reread and remember that question, then go on to the next one.

You are looking for *give-aways*. A give-away occurs when the answer to one question appears in the wording of another question. This happens occasionally; don't miss it.

One question might read: "How many phases does the moon go through in one cycle?" Later on, you may find a question like this: "Of the four phases of the moon, which has the greatest gravitational effect on earth?"

Questions can contain answers. Don't get so involved with individual questions that you miss the interaction between questions. By reviewing the questions first, you are more likely to catch give-aways. This is rare, but it's free. Take it.

Another reason to read all the questions is to make sure you understand all the questions. Don't blow points by answering the wrong question. If you see ambiguity in a question, ask the professor to resolve it. If he won't, then it is a simple question. Look for the simplest answer.

You know the questions and the relative point values. Now it's strategy time.

It is extremely unusual to receive a test that is too long to finish in the given time period. Most exams rate quality, not quantity. Usually, students who are still working at the end of the test period either do not know the material or they are mindlessly adhering to the credo of the herd: Unused test time lowers your grade.

I am a slow writer and a very slow reader, yet my average time to complete an exam was approximately 65% of the allotted period. My average score on those exams was roughly 94%. That's without a curve.

It wasn't magic. I had studied ahead and worked in class. I knew the material. It doesn't take long to complete an exam when you know the answers.

However, to be on the safe side, plan to get the most points in the least amount of time. There are two kinds of questions: instant questions and essay questions. Consider them separately.

Instant questions

Instant questions have one indisputable answer. True/False, multiple choice, and fill-in-the-blank are types of instant questions. You cannot get fancy with instant questions. The answers are either right or wrong.

The larger the class size, the more instant questions you will see. Why? Because someone has to grade them. No one wants to read and grade 157 essay tests.

Many people offer tricks to help you answer these questions. "Longer questions are true," and "If you see the word 'always' or 'never' it is false" are examples. Don't use these tricks. They were created for the uneducated.

Your professor has a Ph.D. She may not be nice or pleasant or considerate, but she is not stupid. Do you honestly think a person could receive a doctorate degree and not know these tricks?

As often as is possible, base answers on your knowledge. Read the questions carefully and answer the question that was asked. Don't assume things about the question that aren't written there. Don't make the test harder than it is.

During your initial reading of the questions, answer every instant question about which you are certain. Be decisive. If you know the answer, put it down and move on. Don't second guess yourself.

If you don't know the answer, move on anyway. You have plenty of time if you don't waste it.

Never spend time on an instant question until you have reviewed all the other questions. Instant questions are the lowest point questions. They are not worth extra time that might be used for other questions you haven't seen yet.

Be definitive. Don't try to write T's that look like F's. Don't mark several answers on a multiple choice. Write legibly when answering fill-in-the-blanks. Unreadable answers will be resolved against you.

They're on to you. Don't make them think you are trying to get away with something. Getting an answer wrong is no big deal. Making a professor think you are being tricky can hurt your subjective grade. That can really cost you.

Here are some tips:

True/False. When you put down an answer, justify it to yourself. If you can explain the part of the question that makes your answer clear, you have the right answer. If not, you are guessing.

Multiple choice. Read the answers first, before you read the question. You should know why your answer is right. You should also know why the other answers are wrong. If you don't know both of these things, think it through again.

Fill-in-the-blank. Put down the correct answer. There isn't much else to do here, except look for give-aways.

If there is no correction factor, don't leave any question unanswered.

A *correction factor* is a grading method where some percentage of the wrong answers is subtracted from the correct answers. Is there a correction factor on your test? Find out!

If not, guess away.

If so, what is it? It will usually be expressed as a fraction (e.g., 1/4 or 1/3). If you can narrow your choices to fewer than the bottom number of the fraction (the denominator), take a guess. Always guess on true/false questions. It's even money.

With a 1/4 correction factor, guess on all questions you can narrow down to fewer than four answers. If you can only narrow it down to four answers, you can guess anyway, but your expectation is zero on these questions. You will learn this if you take a probability course.

Instant questions should be dealt with instantly. Answer when you know; skip them when you don't. Be sure to see all the questions before going back to any of them. You might catch a give-away, and that will save you time.

Be decisive.

Be definitive.

Essay questions

Essay questions are a whole different ball game. Here you have latitude. Here you can get fancy. Here you can get away with murder, but you have to plan it carefully.

Essays are not clear-cut like instant questions. Essays are resolved with the subjective grade. If you have prepared the professor properly, she already believes you know the answer. Don't contradict her.

Many essays have been written about how to write essays. It won't hurt you to read them. Here are some standard points about handling essays:

Read the questions first. Read carefully and simply. There are no trick essay questions. Trick questions usually are instant questions. Don't look for tricks in essay questions.

An essay is a small paper. It is an argument. You must make a conclusion and defend it. That's easy.

On your first pass through the questions, write your conclusions. Now run through them again and estimate how long each defense will be. It doesn't have to be long. Length has nothing to do with points. In fact, if the professor thinks you are rambling unintelligibly, you will lose points.

To estimate the length, write a brief outline on scratch paper. Two or three points should suffice. Be brief and clear.

Now go back and answer the questions, starting with the shortest and proceeding to the longest. This is the most time-effective approach.

Each sentence you write should take some part of the question directly to your conclusion. The question should appear in your answer. Remember this: Each sentence you write must lead inevitably to your conclusion. Check your answer and see if it does.

Use the terminology of the course in your answer. Do not misuse terminology! Both points are imperative.

You must explain your answer in terms of the vocabulary of the subject. This won't be a problem if you've read the chapter on studying.

Remember: Essays are not written. They are constructed.

Write clearly and legibly. If they can't read it, it's wrong. Print if you have poor penmanship. Scribbling an answer is just as impressive as mumbling in class, and you'll get just as much credit.

"Essays are not written. They are constructed."

Be conversant. Write the essay as if you are talking to the professor. Know why? Because you are. Don't be stiff. Be objective and direct.

Above all else, be concise. Don't dawdle in making a point. Whether or not you know what you are talking about, be concise.

What is the single most irritating thing for a professor reading an essay? It's the feeling he should be using a shovel instead of a pencil. Got it? Good.

If possible, use your personal knowledge of the professor to support your answer.

Have you been doing your office hour visits? If you have, some chatting should have occurred. Did you pay attention? Did you learn the professor's point of view on things? Her likes and dislikes? Use it. Don't regurgitate. Use their perspective. The first time I did, it was an accident.

I had an in-class essay in freshman lit. I hated freshman lit. We had to analyze Young Goodman Brown, an allegorical extravaganza.

There was a great deal of vivid imagery in this story. Wandering into the deep dark woods. Witches dancing around. Flames rising and falling. Then a spectacular climax in which water shoots forth from some rock. Then suddenly, all is still, dark, and quiet. At least that's what I remember.

I knew this professor was sexually obsessed. It was more than apparent from his in-class lectures. So I wrote what I thought was a completely sarcastic essay on how this story was a metaphor for sexual intercourse. I took each part of the action in the story and explained how it represented some part of the physical act of love.

It was a lark. I was sick of the class. I thought it would be funny, for me, so I did it. I was not, at all times, the brightest person in school.

I handed in the essay and left. As soon as I got out of the building, I laughed non-stop for half an hour. I knew it was a stupid thing to do, but what the hell. It was fun letting loose. Sometimes you go with your heart over your head. I figured I could take one F and not kill my B. There was no way I was getting an A in that class, and I knew it.

When I got the paper back, the grade was a C+. I read the comments. He had given me a split grade. An F for grammar and syntax (mine was atrocious), and an A+ for concept. He wrote: "This is the most interesting interpretation of YGB I have ever read. Grammar and syntax pull your grade down unfairly."

I laughed for another half hour.

I was a freshman then, just beginning to catch on to the RASABIC system. This "accident" taught me a valuable lesson. It was no accident that I used it effectively from then on.

When you know how a professor likes to view things, answer from that point of view. Don't regurgitate. Emulate.

Getting credit for garbage

Here is a non-standard point that you won't find in many places: How to get credit for garbage answers.

It should never happen that you read a question and don't understand the terms or the idea. If you've been reading and attending class, nothing will be unheard of.

However, it is possible to read a question and draw a complete blank on the answer. It won't happen often. In fact, it may never happen. If it does though, think about this:

You can't start spewing random thoughts and unrelated terms and hope for credit. You won't get any, and you don't deserve any.

You can, however, form a logical and methodical approach to an answer that doesn't exist. This *is* worth something. It shows you are thinking, and that is what professors want to see.

How do you do it? By applying the methodology of the subject to the question. Remember the discussion of methodology in the previous chapter? Here is one place to use it.

Methodology should appear in your discussions for other questions as well. The difference is you knew where you were going with those questions. This time you don't.

Think of the explanations you've been studying. How did the authors approach the problems? What was their line of reasoning? What were the key terms they used to analyze those problems? Now take their approach and repeat it with this question.

You're going to have to think it through, but you can do it. Start applying the methodology to the question and make a logical argument. You might even wind up with the right answer, but even if you don't, it's OK. The professor will recognize that you are reasoning in the subject. He will be impressed. You have a leg to stand on.

Now the subjective grade comes in. If you have laid a solid basis and gained the benefit of the doubt, you will start getting credit. Either the professor will see your reasoning and give substantial partial credit for this display, or he will not be able to follow exactly what you are doing and presume you are right and give full credit.

That's right, full credit.

Professors don't always understand what you are writing. There are correct answers, there are wrong answers, and then there is the gray zone of answers that might be right.

Using sound methodology in your answer can get you into the gray zone. A positive subjective grade will get you credit.

When a professor thinks you might be right, he asks this simple question: Does this student know the material? Your subjective grade is the answer to this question.

Believe it. This has worked for me a number of times in college. It was rare that I had no idea what the answer was, but never did I receive half credit or less on any essay question. That made a lot of borderline tests A's instead of B's.

Don't forget your question prospecting. Anything you learned during these exercises may well be applicable here. The professor will remember it too.

By the way, don't even attempt these questions until you have finished the rest of the exam.

Here are your graded tests

When you get your test back, you are still not done. The postmortem on the test holds valuable information.

First, make sure you understand exactly how you missed every point that you did. Even if you made a 99. Reconstruct your test so it would be a perfect 100 if you handed it back in. This will be a study guide later.

Next, pay careful attention to the professor as the test is reviewed. If you hear the professor say: "A lot of you missed this one," or "I was very disappointed with the answers to number ...," mark that question clearly and be sure you have a perfect answer for it. You will see that question again, I guarantee.

When a professor is particularly disappointed with the response to one question, he goes on a mission to make that point clear. This mission will culminate in the question being re-asked, either verbatim or with a slight modification. Count on it.

After class, look back through your notes and find the questions you had marked with a big "T." These were your guesses for the likely test questions. How did you do?

If you were right on, excellent. If not, how many did you have? Find the answers to those questions in your notes. Do you remember how that material was emphasized during the lecture? Use this opportunity to hone your skill at predicting test questions. It is an art worth cultivating.

Lastly, ask yourself: Was it a good test?

Don't ask yourself: Did I do well?

Ask yourself: Was it a good test?

Did it cover the material thoroughly? How many trick questions were there? What does this test say about the professor? What was stressed, and what was overlooked?

Was it a good test for the material it was supposed to have covered?

Here is a story you may not believe, but I swear it is true:

I was taking an upper level calculus course. The professor gave his fourth test of the semester. It was a true/false test. Ten questions, each worth ten points.

I was really upset because at that level, a true/false test is absurd. The point is to examine the approach to the problems, not to simply match up final answers.

I went into that test carrying a 98.6 average. Everyone in the class scored either a 60, a 70, or an 80. I got a 70.

I went to the professor during office hours and complained. I asked why he gave a true/false test in advanced calculus. He told me he was trying to make it easier on the grader.

I explained my feeling that this was not an appropriate consideration. Why should the students care about the grader? The students should care about an adequate opportunity to demonstrate their knowledge, and nothing else.

I went on to say that this test was not an accurate measure of knowledge. I made this point by telling him that if I got a 70, it couldn't be accurate. I know what you are thinking. I could hardly believe it myself.

I insisted that my 70 was proof that the test was no good since I knew the material. I demanded a re-test.

Guess what? He agreed. He knew I knew the material and he also knew he was copping out by giving a test like that. Of course, he never expected to be called on it, but professors are reasonable people. If you make a valid case, they will treat you fairly.

He gave another test. I got a 99. I didn't complain about that one.

I don't have to tell you that the class was overjoyed at this turn of events, but this is not a popularity contest. I believed in what I was doing, and the professor agreed. He did not go through all that just to mollify me; of this there is no doubt.

I'm not suggesting you blame the professor or the test for bad grades, but it may happen that you feel a test was given unfairly or inadequately.

If you really believe you are right, don't be afraid to follow through. If your point is valid, the professor will probably see it and deal with it. Have a little faith in these people. You're entrusting them with your brain.

Another point of this story is that working on your subjective grade does not mean being a kiss-ass. I certainly wasn't kissing ass by telling the professor his test sucked and should be redone.

I did, however, make a valid point that reinforced his feeling that I knew the material and understood the methodology of the subject. This helped my subjective grade.

Recommendation: Be very good before attempting this one.

Finals

My favorite time of year. I did less work during finals than at any other time during the term. When you know the course material, you know the course material. Studying becomes redundant and pedantic, so you do less of it.

Use your tests from the term. You should be able to get 100% on every test given so far.

Review your notes. Look at all the "T" and "F" questions you have marked throughout the term. Know all these questions and answers intimately.

Revisit all your lists. Concentrate on the items you keep missing until you know them all.

Reread your highlighting. Recall the explanations from the text and the lectures. Relive the term in your mind. This doesn't take that long.

Stay away from the dormitory. People are freaking out. Some students take pride in the demonstration of their freaking out. Don't get involved in this.

They are going nuts, and you are not the kind of company their misery loves. Just stay clear and keep a relatively low profile.

Don't worry about multiple finals in one day. Here is a true story. It happened to me:

At the end of one term, I wound up with three finals in one day. The school policy was that a student could only be required to take two finals in one day. It was my prerogative to reschedule one final if I wanted.

The day before THE day, my brother (who had stolen my mother's car and run away, evading a thirteen-state dragnet chosen especially for him) showed up at my dorm room with the car.

I figured I had enough to deal with, so I went to my professor and asked to reschedule his exam. He wouldn't do it.

I told him it was my prerogative to do it. He just smiled and said: "Howard, take the exam. See how you do."

It was not, in my opinion, the best idea to attempt three exams with everything else going on. Dealing with my brother had cost me review time which I thought I needed. I was wrong.

I scored 97.5% on the morning exam, 100% on the afternoon exam, and a cool 96% on the evening exam (the one I attempted to reschedule). I was an exam stud.

I learned that I knew the material better than I thought. We are all trained to believe we must study to do well. That is true, but no one says when that studying must take place.

By working early and consistently throughout the term, you will know the material. You will know it cold!

If you have done the groundwork, some solid review is all you'll need for finals.

Relax for finals, but don't fall asleep completely. See a movie. Read a book. Review your material lightly and regularly. You are going to ace the final. If you use RASABIC, you won't be able to avoid it.

Papers

Papers are nothing more than big essay questions. Don't make a big deal out of them.

Reread the section on essay questions (earlier in this chapter). Remember to have a clear conclusion and to keep moving toward that conclusion with your argument.

Outline your approach, and research it. As you increase the detail of the outline, the paper will virtually write itself.

Organization and structure are the essence of a good paper.

Always type your papers. Neatness does count. Blow a dollar on a report cover. A few simple touches can make a big difference.

There are many subtleties to college papers. There is a plethora of good material available on writing college papers. Read it if you feel you need it. It couldn't hurt.

The most important thing to keep in mind about papers is this: Grading papers is the most subjective exercise there is for a professor. Your subjective grade will weigh heavily in the outcome. If you are in a paper intensive curriculum, work intensely on your subjective grade. It is going to come into play a lot.

Course Selection Scheduling & Graduating Early 8

You now have everything you need to conquer any individual course. This is vital, but it's only a part of the college picture.

This chapter covers how to put those courses together. This chapter gives you the big picture.

A college degree means more than taking a bunch of courses. It means taking the right courses, in the right order. There are requirements to meet if you are to qualify for a degree. You need a plan.

Course handbook

Every entering freshman receives a handbook of courses well before arriving at school. It contains all the courses that are available to you through the college or university. The day you get that booklet is the day you begin to conquer college.

The course handbook contains a lot of information, much more than a listing of courses and descriptions.

Note the organization of the booklet. The courses are arranged by subject. The subjects are arranged by category of study.

There are three general categories of study: Humanities, Social Sciences, and Sciences.

There will be a separate section on degree requirements and other sections on general information.

This is the bible. Keep it handy.

Learning the requirements

First read through the degree requirements. Become intimately familiar with them. Don't make up your own requirements. Just read what's there with an open mind.

You will find three principle types of degree requirements: a general education requirement (for breadth), a major requirement (for depth), and a minimum course work requirement (to keep you paying tuition for four years). There may also be some specific course requirements, such as freshman literature or a language.

Whether in hours, credits, or units, each of these requirements will be specified clearly. They dictate how you must select courses if you are to graduate with a degree.

The general education requirement will give some minimum amount of course work for each of the three general categories of study: Humanities, Social Sciences, and Sciences.

The major requirement will specify some minimum amount of course work for one subject, your major subject.

The minimum course work requirement is just that, the minimum amount of course work you must complete, overall, to graduate.

Now look through the major requirements for several subjects you are likely to choose. You will find them in the beginning of the subject listings, or possibly at the start of a category of study listing.

Know and remember these requirements.

Many students think only in terms of minimum course work requirements. When they find they can't graduate, even though they have completed enough course work, they are very sad.

They whine: "I was planning on graduating now."

They are lying. They did not plan. That is why they aren't graduating.

You must meet all the requirements for graduation, not just one or two. You can't do it if you don't know the requirements.

Course selection

Course Selection is the process of choosing courses toward the ultimate goal of receiving a degree. There are hundreds of thousands of ways to select courses that meet degree requirements. Some take more work, some take a lot less (remember: RASABIC gets the best possible result with the least effort).

With RASABIC, course selection has only two purposes. The first is to meet the requirements for graduation as quickly as possible. The second is to select courses in a way that will minimize study time and maximize your grades. These are the only considerations.

Some might see this as a narrow view of college. I say it is a focused view, the focus being on graduating quickly with a powerful degree. A degree that lets you go where you want to go. A degree that *gives* you options, as opposed to limiting them.

No one cares what courses you took in college. They care how you did in those courses.

When I tell people I graduated in three years with a double major and a 3.9 GPA, they never ask what courses I took. They just say "Wow."

I received many substantial job opportunities from wow-sayers.

Before going on, I would like to take a moment to debunk the three greatest myths of course selection. You will hear them frequently. You should understand why they are myths.

Myth #1: Spread yourself around. Try all kinds of things. College is an intellectual smorgasbord, and it's all you can eat.

Debunk #1: Each time you try an entirely different subject you are starting all over again. By doing this continually, you are spreading yourself very thin. You are never cashing in on your investment in the first course, and you could be getting into completing-your-major trouble.

You are also asking for big weeder courses. *Weeder courses* are intro courses made extra tough to get rid of non-majors. Why do this to yourself?

Myth #2: You've got plenty of time.

Debunk #2: This is the battle cry of the mediocre student, the loser. The more you say this to yourself, the more you will delay making decisions that need to be made early in your college career.

Myth #3: Pick professors, not courses.

Debunk #3: Professors do not fill requirements, courses do. If you can choose between several professors for the same course, then by all means go for it. Otherwise, choose courses.

These myths are fine if you are independently wealthy and are going into the family business after graduation.

RASABIC assumes you are not in this enviable position. RASABIC is not for getting by in college. It's for *conquering college*.

Synergy

In the RASABIC theory of course selection, *synergy* is the secret of selecting and scheduling courses for your speediest, easiest, and most successful graduation.

Synergy means working together. The whole is greater than the sum of the parts.

RASABIC Synergy means taking course groupings and multiple majors. It means letting the courses reinforce one another, just like class work reinforces your studying.

RASABIC Synergy lets the courses do some of the work, so you don't have to.

Let's talk selection.

Pick your majors

Before you start college, you should select your majors. That's right, plural. Pick three majors. One in Science, one in Social Science, and one in Humanities.

The idea is not to settle on one major and drop the others. The idea is to have a multiple major. You will need more than enough courses to do this anyway (minimum course work requirement); why not make that course work reflect something?

I only double majored, with an outside minor. Give me a break. It took a while to figure all this out. You don't have that handicap.

As was said earlier, no one cares what courses you took, but telling people you completed a double major is very impressive. If you complete a triple major, you will need floor padding for peoples' jaws.

Multiple majoring is easy to do. It's just that most students never think of it. It requires the same number of courses. The only difference is in selecting courses in the same subjects instead of spreading the courses around.

It's a much bigger bang for the same college buck.

Pick things you know you like. If you don't know what the subjects are, go to the library and scan through a few books. All the information you need is there. Test them out while you are still in high school. Settle on some subjects and stick with them.

Which major you select is not very important. Really. There are plenty of sociology and philosophy majors in medical school, and there are many biology majors in law school.

The important thing is having a major. This will enable you to focus on selecting courses efficiently for requirement satisfaction. You will not be distracted by extraneous considerations.

Employers don't care too much about what you studied. They figure on training you anyway. Their question is: Can you learn their training? A dynamite college record tells them exactly what they want to know—that you can learn quickly and ably.

Don't keep changing your majors. Many students can't get through because they change their major so often they wind up with no concentration in anything.

The main reason students change majors is not hatred of the subject; it is laziness and a refusal to work. Naturally they are not doing well in their current major, and they eschew (good one, look it up) any responsibility for their lack of effort. Instead, they blame their major and switch, thinking they will do better in another area. Sometimes this works. Most times it doesn't. These are the most panicked students at registration.

Another benefit of starting with three majors is flexibility. If it turns out you genuinely hate one subject, you can drop it and still have two other majors to fall back on. You may even have time to pick up a new third major.

What about requirements? By choosing your majors this way, you don't even have to think about your general education and major requirements. They become automatic.

Lastly, multiple majors give you the maximum opportunity to apply course grouping, which reduces your study time and increases your retention.

What's course grouping?

I'm glad you asked.

Course grouping

Course grouping means taking courses in groups, of course.

Actually, it means taking several courses from the same subject at the same time.

Most students think variety is an important part of course selection for a term. They couldn't be more wrong. All they are doing is making sure they will need the maximum possible study time during the term since nothing they do in one course will help with any of the others.

By taking several courses in the same subject concurrently, you will notice some interplay among them. The playground will be your mind.

If economics is one of your majors, take three econ courses during the same term. You will find that ideas from one course will make the theories in the other courses easier to understand. You may even be able to use work from one class to complete assignments in another. That's a big savings, but be careful here. Don't get lazy.

You will find test answers coming from the other classes too. It will also give you a larger pool to draw from when you don't know an answer. (Remember that discussion from the last chapter?)

"Most students think variety is an important part of course selection. They couldn't be more wrong."

Course grouping will also help you perceive the subject's methodology sooner since you will be immersed in it. You will be very focused on the subject, and you will learn each of the courses more quickly and more completely.

Course grouping enables you to carry a heavier schedule, and that is the key to early graduation. It is less work to take seven courses in two subjects than five courses in five subjects (unless those courses have extremely long reading lists; watch out in the humanities).

Yet another advantage of this approach is starting a class with the benefit of the doubt in your favor. Remember the principle of the subjective grade?

If you apply the RASABIC concepts thoroughly, you are going to develop a rep(utation). Among professors, this rep will be very positive.

Professors in the same department talk to one another. One frequent topic is students. I have taken courses where, on the first day, the professor approached me and said: "You're Howard Warshaw aren't you? Professor Greedygree told me about you. I'm looking forward to having you in the class this term."

What he was really saying was: "Hi there. You are going to ace this course. If you want to blow it, you'll have to start very soon."

That is the best possible first day of class you can have. It only happens in higher level courses as you pursue the same subject.

Group your courses together by subject. Never do extra work that course selection can do for you.

Prerequisites

A *prerequisite* is a course that is required for another course. The prerequisite for Calculus II is Calculus I. If a course has any prerequisites, they will be listed in the handbook.

Prerequisites can interfere with course grouping. Fortunately, most subjects have only one or two intro courses which serve as prerequisites for most of the higher level courses.

Your freshman year should be devoted to taking prerequisites. This will give you freedom to group courses in your sophomore and later years.

Multiple schools

Another thing that can interfere with course grouping is term specific courses. These are courses that are not offered every term. They may only be available every other term or every third term.

You cannot take courses that aren't offered, but you may be able to take courses that are offered in other schools.

A university is a collection of colleges. You are enrolled in one of the colleges, but that doesn't mean you can't take courses in the other colleges and still get credit. Check the courses in all the colleges at your university.

You may find, as I did, that a course you want to take this term isn't offered in your school but is offered in another school. Maybe Engineering, the night school, or a sister school.

"You may find a course you want in another school.
Maybe Engineering, the night school, or a sister school."

Another way to avoid the off-term problem is independent study. I did this occasionally.

Approach the professor who normally teaches the course and ask to take it on independent study. You will meet regularly and get assignments. You have a good reputation in the department. Use it to your advantage.

Professors will grant you this privilege if they feel you are sincere. If you use the RASABIC system, believe me, no one will think you are kidding.

Independent study can help you avoid waiting one or two terms for a course you want now, and it's usually easier than taking the class.

Check these ideas out with an advisor or the dean's office. You have more options available than you think.

Gut courses

A *gut course* is a course you take for an easy A. Every school has a few of these.

There was a biology course in my school entitled "Man, Nature, and Society." The students called it "Man, Cake, and Society." It was widely known to be a gut course.

Be wary of other students' recommendations. Their cake could be your poison.

Also realize that professors don't always enjoy a gut reputation. You never know when they might suddenly decide to change the student perception of their course. You don't want to be there when that happens.

Find your own gut courses. A gut course is one that you can add to an already heavy schedule because it has almost no study price. The easiest way to do it is with courses you already know.

When I had already completed several programming courses in the science/math department, I was able to find an introductory programming course in one of the social sciences. That was a gut course.

I also relieved a humanities credit with a logic course in the philosophy department, after having done plenty of logic work in math already.

Here's a great one: Take a foreign language you already speak. Watch those language requirements. Don't get bitten.

You cannot graduate on gut courses. There simply aren't very many of them. However, by doing this occasionally (I had about four), I removed nearly an entire term from my degree.

People are still impressed with my early graduation. Especially my parents, who helped pay for my college education. No one has ever asked me how many gut courses I took.

Map it out

Knowing all this, go back to the beginning.

You receive your course handbook. Plan your courses from the start. All the way through.

Select your majors. Write down all the prerequisites. This is your freshman schedule.

Don't plan too heavy a schedule for your first term. Take the recommended course load. A lot is going on in the first term. Don't overburden yourself. Concentrate on developing your RASABIC techniques.

Think about course grouping for later years. Take at least three courses in one subject and two in another during each term. Rotate the three-course subject through each of the majors.

Use the handbook to plan your entire college career. You don't have to do it exactly as you plan it, but the experience of having planned it all at least once is a valuable one.

When you run into a glitch in registration (which you will at some point), you will have to make a quick and important decision on the spot. Because you have the planning experience, you know what you need to accomplish with this change. You will avoid many problems that less prepared students deal with frequently.

Pre-register whenever possible

Many colleges offer some form of pre-registration procedure. Use it. It's tough being a course shopper at registration.

You've done your planning. You know what you need. Register in the quickest and simplest way possible.

Incidentally, registration is another big advantage of multiple majoring and course grouping.

When you use the RASABIC theory of course selection, you are taking many more higher level courses than do most students.

Higher level courses are easier to get into than lower level courses. This is because every head of cattle in the registration stampede is mooing, "Try everything. Spread it around." Students never sample higher level courses in an outside subject, only lower level courses.

You will also find higher level courses are easier courses if you learn the prerequisites well, which you will. Precious few students understand this.

Registration

Here are two helpful hints for registration:

➤ Always have one good joke for registration. People become more cooperative if you make them laugh.

➤ Never try to intimidate a bureaucrat, they live to kill intimidators. During registration, the bureaucrats have all the power. Don't make yourself a target.

Graduate early

In the RASABIC school of going to school, early graduation is the BIG WIN!

We live in a fast turn-around, get-it-done society. That's just the way it is. Every potential employer you talk to has some problem on his mind that could be solved by a quick turn-around team. This is how they think.

By graduating early and impressively, you are telling these employers: "Hey, here I am. The answer to your problems. Pay me!"

They will.

You will see how much time you have left over as the term progresses. Use that time as a gauge to determine how many extra courses you could handle next term. If you can handle more, take more. If you find your current schedule is light, add a course now.

Meet your requirements as early as possible. Overload your schedule. As the terms go by, you will master the RASABIC techniques. You will be able to carry heavier loads than most students (and advisors) would recommend. They think about the averages. You are an exception. You are a trained, skilled, collegiate conquistador. You are a college pro.

Don't waste time on an amateur schedule. Go for the gusto.

I didn't have a junior year. At the end of my sophomore year I had a good number of extra credits. By taking a few summer courses, I was able to return in the fall as a senior. I had a junior summer, which cost a lot less than a junior year.

You know how college tuitions are now. How much is a half or a full year's tuition? That is the dollar value of the scholarship RASABIC can grant you. It is entirely in your hands.

By the way, don't forget to submit your degree request on time. You must request a degree in order to graduate. Since you are accelerated, no one will notify you automatically. Seek out this information during your sophomore year and use it.

Scheduling classes

This is pretty simple. Schedule your courses for minimum down time.

Take course blocks. Take courses at 10:00, 11:00, 1:00, and 2:00. Don't take them at 8:00, 11:00, 2:30, and 5:00. Reduce the number of gaps between courses. These are black holes. The easiest way to deal with them is to avoid them.

Take courses when you are best able to perform. If you are a morning person, take the early classes. I was not. I never took a class before 10:00 or 11:00.

Do what you want to do. You know best. Trust yourself.

For those of you who just walked in

☆ Plan. Plan. Plan.

☆ Start when you first get that course handbook.

☆ Choose one major in each area of study. Gear up for that impressive multiple major.

☆ Get your prerequisites out of the way.

☆ After your first term, if you are getting the hang of RASABIC, start overloading your schedule.

☆ Use course grouping to reduce your term studying requirements.

☆ Find out what options are available to you, and . . .

☆ Plan. Plan. Plan.

☆ Pre-register when possible.

☆ Take course blocks to avoid black holes.

☆ Are you getting close to eliminating a term or a year?

☆ Take the occasional gut.

☆ Consider the other schools as well as independent study.

☆ Plan. Plan. Plan.

☆ You need the course work anyway. Do it with multiple majors.

☆ Graduate early for the big pay-off!!!

Final Points & Perspectives

9

Negotiation

Negotiation is the art of asking and receiving. The biggest problem with negotiation in college is that students don't do it.

Never be afraid to ask for something. Anything you and the college agree to becomes official. You cannot take advantage of this if you don't try. The worst that can happen is to be refused, leaving you exactly where you already are. The best that can happen is being able to do what you want, how you want, and get credit for it.

Ask for independent study if you prefer.

If you are on the borderline, ask to be moved up.

If you don't like an assignment, ask to do a different one.

Ask for extra credit work to increase your edge.

Seek credit for outside work you may have done.

Ask to change your curriculum, or make up your own.

You can ask for anything you want. The better your grades, the more likely your request will be granted.

You have seen examples throughout this book of asking for and receiving special options. There is nothing special about that. The school serves you, not the other way around.

Keep this in mind: They can't serve you if you don't ask.

Advisors

Advisors are excellent resources, but nothing more. Do not look to them for direction. Be your own guide.

You alone should do the job of choosing your goals. Advisors are for answering the questions you discover as you do that job.

Advisors can give you information on requirements, courses, curriculum options, and better still, they can teach you how to find these things yourself. Always try to be as self-reliant as possible.

Advisors are like encyclopedias; they don't do you much good until you know what you want. Once you know this, they are very useful.

I never actually met my advisor, and that never posed a problem with my college career. Other students used them often.

Use advisors to help you plan a path. Do not use advisors to choose a path. This is not a slam on advisors. They are fine and knowledgeable people. However, like anyone else, there is little point in asking them to do a job they cannot do.

The answer trap

Disclaimer: Helping other students is a decent and wonderful thing to do. This next discussion is not intended to suggest otherwise. These are just a few things to consider, particularly if you are the kind of person who has trouble saying no:

As you become known as a "good student," you will find classmates seeking you out around test time. Be careful. Don't fall into the *answer trap*.

The potential for crammers to suck up your time is unlimited. You are under no obligation to deal with any of them. When someone asks you for help, ask yourself these three questions:

1. How has this person treated me up to this point?
2. How much time do I have to spend on this?
3. How much do I want to know/date this person?

If you don't find favorable answers to at least two of these questions, you probably shouldn't spend the time.

Wait a second. Before writing them off, there are two other questions worth consideration:

The first question is: Could I use some work in this subject?

The best way to learn is to teach. If you feel a little shaky in this subject, the act of helping someone else may improve your understanding of the material. This is one time a study partner can really help.

If you can make another student understand the material, you will know it quite well yourself. Even if they don't get it, your comprehension is likely to improve.

The second question is: What can this person do for me?

This person has opened a negotiation with you by seeking your help. You are certainly entitled to reciprocation. They may have something you want. Why not ask? They did.

You can get show tickets, meals, tutoring fees, dates, etc.

A "good student" reputation can get you more than grades.

Professor = brain + ego

There are two things you can assume about anyone with a Ph.D. They have a sharp mind and a big ego.

There are plenty of brilliant people with very little ego, and there are too many egotistical people with no smarts. Earning a Ph.D. requires both brains and ego.

The point is: Never treat professors like they are stupid. Don't patronize them or condescend to them.

First, it's rude and uncalled for.

Second, it's committing scholastic suicide with your subjective grade.

Professors have both brains and ego. They are smart enough to see exactly what you are doing, and they are egotistical enough to take real offense over it. Once offended, they are smart enough to take it out on you in ways you cannot deal with.

Professors are wonderful friends and dangerous adversaries. They may not always earn your praise, but they deserve your respect.

Having respect for someone does not preclude disagreeing with them, or even arguing heatedly with them. It means always treating their point of view as being valid and worthy of consideration. It means being courteous and diplomatic, yet not sycophantic (check the glossary; you'll like this word).

Show respect whenever you deal with a professor. You'll never regret it.

Do it now

The only thing you should put off until later is procrastinating.

It is the professor's responsibility to assign work. It is your responsibility to do it.

It is not the professor's responsibility to remind you, or hound you, or check your progress.

You will be assigned papers many weeks in advance. You won't hear about them again until a few days before they are due. If you forget, you fail. It's that simple.

Here is the simple solution: Don't forget!

Start all assignments as soon possible. You can always add to them as the time goes on.

By starting the assignment right away, you will understand exactly what is involved. Anything you are missing can be cleared up by the professor.

If you don't know which way to go with a paper, you can use your class time to ask questions. Clever questions. Questions which don't seem to relate exactly to the lecture but do relate to your paper. You can make the professor write some of your paper without even knowing it.

You can't fish for this kind of information if you don't know what you're looking for, and you can't know what you're looking for until you start the assignment. So start the assignment.

Organizational tools

Two things you are likely to need are a BIG calendar and a weekly schedule.

The weekly schedule is simple. Write seven columns on a sheet of paper. Each column represents one day of the week. Block out your classes and activities on this sheet. This will give you a visual image of your week and help you plan your study time more effectively.

The BIG calendar is for marking the dates of tests and papers, so you won't forget about them.

Check these two documents often. Always be aware of time. Time is the only limiting factor you will face. Make sure you face it.

Senior anxiety (Pre-partum depression)

Senior anxiety is a phenomenon in which seniors become depressed and morose for seemingly no reason.

This is difficult for an underclassman to understand. Seniors should be happy because they are about to get out.

Paradoxically, the reason they are sad is because they are about to get out.

They have not created a degree that will serve them in the future. They have created a non-stop party haven, which is great while it lasts.

Unfortunately, the end is now in sight. Reality is crashing in on them as they realize that the last three or four years were not about partying; those years were about the future. And now it's the future.

College has been great for them. More accurately, being in college has been great for them. They had a lot of fun and didn't have to worry about much of anything, until now.

Now they have to face the fact they are unprepared to move on from college. This is a very depressing fact to face.

Don't empathize with them, learn from them. Learn from their mistakes.

There are two kinds of happy seniors; good-job recipients and graduate school scholarship winners. The rest are oozing desperation from every pore.

RASABIC will ensure that you never fall prey to senior anxiety. You will realize my uncle's wisdom when he said: "In college, if you get good grades, you have a good time."

Cheating

Don't do it. Ever! You won't need to.

If someone offered you the opportunity to ruin your entire college career, and possibly a good deal of your professional life, for no gain, what would you tell them?

Frats & Sororities (Brother, can you spare that dime in your nose?)

I know what I hate, and I don't hate fraternities. Here are a few salient facts:

Frats and sororities take up your time. If you join, you will have obligations to meet. Your time will not be entirely your own.

Your brothers and sisters rarely want to help you study, or even *see* you study for that matter.

They will always provide compelling alternatives to studying, and compelling reasons to go along.

They have great rush parties.

When talking to Greeks (the generic term for fraternities and sororities, derived from their names which use Greek letters), ask them about the house average. The house average is the cumulative average of all the grades in the membership. Whatever they tell you, subtract at least 0.3 from it.

Now ask yourself: Is this a GPA I'd be proud of?

They will tell you of their sister who is carrying a 4.0. There are people who can party all the time—not just every night—and still make the grades. There is a name for these people: Genius.

I'm not a genius. Are you?

They will tell you how they have every test from every professor in the school. They will tell you how they can save you tremendous amounts of study time—time that can be used for Greek functions.

They are not referring to RASABIC, and they are not all Dean's list candidates.

Greeks are about having fun. They are about extending your adolescence into your twenties. They are a support organization, and a good one. They are about feeling like you belong.

The question is: What will you belong to?

I am not saying it is wrong to join a Greek organization. I am saying that you should not kid yourself about what you are doing. There are very few serious students in frats and sororities. There are some, but not many.

Greeks cannot make you do poorly in college. Only you can do that. Greeks can, however, provide a very convenient and tempting environment for failure.

Every fraternity and sorority has a few great students. No fraternity or sorority is composed exclusively of great students.

Greeks can be superior students, but this requires either amazing brain power, or amazing discipline and a remarkable liver.

Good college advice: *"When you are already dizzy and nauseous, you don't need another Tequila Shooter."*

The social test

Many people position college as a major social test. Don't let this distract you. This is only true if you make it so.

Don't lose sight of your goal: to graduate as impressively as possible. While in college, your job is to do as well as possible *in college*.

Whether or not you go to college, you will have to deal with people. Being popular has very little to do with succeeding in college. You will never see the following question on a job application or hear it in an interview: Were you popular in college?

If you haven't learned social skills in high school, you will have plenty of time after college. Decide if you want to learn them in a lousy job or a good one.

The need to belong is a strong one. Consider what you want to belong to.

Do you want to belong to the "crowd?" The crowd gets B's and C's. You don't want to "fit in" there.

Do you want to belong to the group that succeeds in college and parlays that success into the professional arena? If so, don't worry about social tests. Worry about college exams.

How to make it tougher than it is

There are two primary ways to make college more difficult:

1. Forgetting your purpose
2. Looking for short cuts

Never forget your purpose: conquering college. You are there to succeed and reap the benefits. Having fun is a nice bonus, one you will enjoy regularly, but fun is not your purpose.

The key to succeeding is to remain focused on the swift completion of your goal. College is full of tempting distractions, which is why few people succeed. They lack the discipline to stay focused in this environment. Don't get distracted. Always remember the reason you are there: to succeed.

Looking for short cuts can hurt you. You now have the RASABIC system. All aspects of RASABIC work together to get you the best possible grades with the minimum effort.

The RASABIC system *is* a short cut. It is the big picture. Don't try to cut it any further until you use and understand it.

Stick with it. At times, especially at first, it will not seem like a short cut. It will seem like you are doing a lot of work while your classmates are doing little or nothing.

You will see later—if you do stick with it—that suddenly all your classmates are running around panicked while you are doing very little and having a good time.

They have fun while their grades are still in the air. You have fun while your grades are secure. Your way is more fun.

Understand how it works for you. Give it at least two terms. Then adjust it as you like.

Some realities for the aggressive student

Unfortunately, there are many small people. I don't mean short. I mean petty.

There is a disease that infects human beings. This disease is called "Evasion of Responsibility." College students are particularly susceptible.

When you go to college, you are there to study and make grades. That is your responsibility as a student. It is the unspoken contract you sign upon entry.

Many students evade this responsibility. They refuse to accept it. If you take a psychology course, you will learn that the name for this is "denial."

So what? Everyone is free to choose in college. One available choice is not to participate.

Many students will make this choice, and that's fine. They are welcome to it, and they will face the consequences. That has nothing to do with you. They make their choice and you make yours.

What *does* have to do with you is their reaction. They are not doing well, and seeing you do well will remind them of this fact. They will blame you for making them feel badly and they will resent you. This is what I mean by petty.

They will do no more than give you dirty looks and the occasional snide comment, but it is unpleasant.

You will not receive this feedback from other good students, just from poor students who lack the maturity to take responsibility for their own actions.

You can appease these people by doing worse and making them feel better, but I recommend against this. I also recommend not laughing out loud when they seek your help around finals.

Take responsibility for yourself

When you miss things, accept the fact that *you* did it. Then take the steps necessary to prevent that failure from recurring.

Likewise, when you succeed, revel in the fact that *you* did it. Pat yourself on the back. Don't pretend you got lucky, or that some mistake was made. Realize that your work and dedication paid off. Enjoy it. You earned it.

In college, you are the sole determinant of your outcome. This is a rare situation in life. Don't evade it. Embrace it.

Forgive yourself

When you grow up and take responsibility for yourself, successes taste sweeter and failures are more bitter.

As a collegiate conquistador you will win the war, but it is unlikely you will win every battle. There are times when it just won't happen for you.

You must be able to forgive your failures and move on to other successes. I faced this right at the start of my freshman year.

There was no way I was going to ace freshman lit, and I knew it. My grammar and syntax really were horrible (that professor might have been sexually obsessed, but he had me pegged grammatically). What made it worse yet was the fact that freshman lit was two required courses, not just one.

So I accepted this and just made sure I got at least B's. I finished my freshman year with a 3.78 GPA. As you read in Chapter 1, this was my worst annual GPA in college.

I never lost my resolve to be the best where I could, even in the face of two sure failures right up front (I considered B's failures. C's never even occurred to me after high school, where I had plenty of them).

Forgiveness is a very important part of responsibility. If you can't do something completely, do the best you can and move on.

Don't beat yourself up. That will only detract from the things you can do completely.

You don't belong in college

That's right, and it is a very important point. You do not belong in college.

College is merely a stepping stone on the way to where you do belong.

Don't look past college and lose your way. Focus intently on college while you are there.

Simply remember that it is only a means to an end. Your ultimate goals lie far beyond the campus.

Do it again

If you have not yet been to college or are currently a freshman on your first reading of this book, plan on rereading it after your first two terms.

Theory is a lovely thing, but it can be difficult to understand many of these concepts fully without some real-life experience.

Most of the advice in this book is straightforward and directly applicable. However, some of the techniques and ideas are more subtle. They will require some time and thought to administer completely.

After you have spent some time in college, reread this book. I guarantee you will gain insights and techniques that you missed the first time through.

This is high-density information. The more you sift through it the more you will find.

This is it

I had a stellar college career, and I did it my way. I didn't do what they told me to do. I showed them what I could do, using their rules.

You can do it too. I'm no better than you are. There is a lot of flexibility in college. There are more requirements, but there are also fewer regulations.

Most students don't bother to familiarize themselves with all of their options in college. Don't make this mistake.

This book is full of advice. But if I had to choose only one piece of advice to give to college students, this would be it:

> The less you know about a system, the less you are able to manipulate it. The better you understand a system, the more you can exploit the system to your own advantage.

> College is a system. Don't be afraid of the system. Learn it intimately. Know everything you can about the system. Then use your knowledge mercilessly to

Conquer College.

Glossary

ace (a course)   To get an "A," or the highest grade in a course.

automaton   A person who acts in a machine-like way, with no feeling or awareness. A joyless robot.

bifurcation   A splitting of something into two parts or branches.

chagrin   Sadness or disappointment.

connotation   An idea or meaning, other than the obvious or explicit ones, that is suggested by a word or phrase. In other words, a bonus interpretation.

cramming   The willful and malicious act of trying to make your short term memory do something it was never intended to do. Stuffing your head with facts for a test.

credo   A deeply held principle or belief.

curve   A term used in grading tests. It means that each test is graded relative to the class average score on the test, rather than the absolute point total. For example, if the class average is 43%, a grading curve could make a test score of 65% an "A," as opposed to a "D" or worse.

Dean's list   The honor roll of top students (according to grades) for each individual term.

decibel   A unit of measurement for sound. The more decibels, the louder the sound.

defenestration   The throwing of something out a window, like yourself for instance.

edification   Enlightenment, instruction, improvement.

eschew   Bless you (just kidding). To avoid or shun. To stay away from.

expository   Explanatory or informational. Having the quality of showing or demonstrating something. The definitions in this glossary are expository. That last sentence is not only expository, it is self-referential.

finals   This is short for "final examinations." It refers to the period of time at the end of the term when nearly every student on campus is sweating because the last (and most significant) tests in each course are being given. It is also used to refer to the individual tests.

frat   Short for fraternity. Fraternities are social organizations that can make your life fuller, as well as your bladder and liver.

freshman   A first year student in a four-year college.

greek   A term that refers to fraternities, sororities, or their members. It connotes the fact that these organizations use Greek letters for their names.

hermetically   Locked in, airtight, completely sealed.

highlighter   A marker which has brightly colored translucent ink. It is used to paint certain passages in a textbook so that they stand out clearly when reviewing the text.

highlighting   The act of using a highlighter, as opposed to merely the intention of using one.

inexorably   Unavoidably, relentlessly, irresistibly.

libido Typically used to refer to the sexual urge or instinct. In psychoanalytic terms, it is used to refer to the basic driving force behind all human action. Do you think so?

lit Short for literature.

junior A third year student in a four-year college.

malleable Adaptable, yielding, able to be reformed.

matriculate To register or enroll in a college or university, or the act of attending said institution with intention of graduating or receiving a degree.

midterms Just like finals, only the exams are not quite as significant in your grade (they are still very significant). These tests occur in the middle of the term, hence the name.

Nirvana A state of inner peace and high consciousness. It's good!

pedantic A narrow-minded insistence on exact adherence to a set of arbitrary rules. Also the exaggeration of the importance of minor or trivial points of learning.

plethora A great deal (as in quantity, not as in shopping).

pristine Pure, uncorrupted, unspoiled.

quad A quad is any large open grassy area on a college campus. This is short for quadrangle, which is the usual shape.

salient Significant, noticeable, prominent.

senior A fourth year student in a four-year college.

sophomore A second year student in a four-year college.

subliminally Beneath the threshold of conscious perception. When something affects you without your awareness, it has affected you subliminally.

sycophantic   To behave in such a manner as to give the clear and unmistakable impression of kissing ass.

syllabus   An outline or summary of the main topics to be covered in a course. Should also contain the dates and descriptions of tests and papers, as well as necessary course materials.

synergy   The combined or co-operative action of two or more individual things.

Valhalla   Viking heaven.

Index

R

S

T

W

Notes

Notes

Notes

Notes

Would you like to give the gift that keeps on giving?

To obtain a copy of Conquering College for yourself or a friend, either inquire at your local bookstore, or write to us directly at:

EduQuest Corporation
P.O. Box 610787
San Jose, CA   95161-0787

Please include check or money order for $15.95 ($12.95 cover price plus $3.00 shipping and handling). Foreign orders add an additional $2.00 for postage, please.

CA residents include $1.00 sales tax or a valid resale number with order.

Multiple book orders qualify for quantity discounts. Please call us at (408) 441-7355 for discount information.